THE KILT
FOR
KEEPS

THE KILT FOR KEEPS

GIDEON SCOTT MAY

Drawings by
PETER MOONIE

Alloway Publishing

Alloway Publishing Ltd
Hastings Square Darvel
Ayrshire Scotland

Revised Edition 1993 published by Alloway Publishing

First published at Croft Douglas, Strathtummel, Pitlochry, 1983

Copyright © Gideon Scott May 1983

ISBN 0-907526-59-4

Designed and printed by Walker & Connell Ltd.
and The Cromwell Press

To My Kilted Grandsons

1

Life began when I discovered the delicate secret of balance, and mastered the art of standing up.

My mother seemed to have waited for this moment. She was fiercely proud of being a Scot, loved life and its colours, and had a passion for the tartan. After a frantic search around my podgy middle for the slightest semblance of a waistline, she determinedly strapped a miniature MacDonald, Clanranald, kilt around me. A picture hangs in my mind of mother kneeling beside me with arms akimbo, fists dug deeply into her waist, and her eyes aglitter with excitement as she appraised her handiwork. Then she wrapped her arms around me and I felt a warm, questioning, whisper in my ear:

"You will wear it for me?"

I sensed the importance of the question and nodded my head.

"Always?"

I knew already what it was to be loved but hadn't consciously given any in return, nor was able to speak of it, so I just nodded my head again and hoped it would keep the laughter in her eyes. The kilt immediately gave me two things; a warm, secure, support around my middle and, when my legs tired and buckled at the knees, the thick, tartan pleats provided a happy landing.

On my next birthday I was presented with a sporran, a young badger with a cleancut black and white striped head, golden glowing eyes and a 'please get to know me' expression. The little badger was truly my best friend. In company I had only to look upwards and brace myself for the reaction which ranged from a delicate pat on the head, a hefty masculine thump, a nervous poke from a maiden aunt to the soft stroking from an understanding hand and always, always, the coin that my little badger soon learned to devour greedily.

The sporran led me into a glorious disregard of monetary value as was fully demonstrated when I was asked to be a page at a family wedding. For this event my kilt was topped off with a rich green velvet doublet, a frothy, white, jabot around my neck with matching laces around my wrists. My appearance, carrying the bride's train was greeted with a chorus of "Oohs" and "Aahs" from the guests. These quickly changed to an outsized gasp of alarm when I tripped, but anxiety turned to hilarity when the bride, who was a buxom lass, made light of the extra load as she towed me along on my tummy!

Somehow I managed to regain my feet, some composure, and completed my journey to the altar in command of the tail of the bride's train.

After the wedding ceremony and amidst a multi-coloured snowstorm of confetti, the bride and bridegroom left the church and I watched, wide-eyed, as the Best Man reached into his pocket and threw a handful of coins to the waiting children. I marvelled at the resulting chaos; the welter of bodies, tangling, struggling, biting, kicking and fighting for the money. Peace was restored only when the clawing hands had grabbed the final penny.

It was then I put my hand down the badger's throat and, casting the contents of its insides to the crowd, gleefully watched the fiendish fighting all over again.

The kilt I had now accepted as my daily dress, for the simple reason I had nothing else to put on but, at that time, the other children took me as I was. Dress and sex being immaterial we played the days away quite happily. Happily, that was, until it was time for the fledgling to leave the nest to learn, in the main, about life and other living creatures.

At school, my kilt drew the hoots, jeers and jostlings of the other boys. I was like an owl blinking bewilderedly at this sudden attack in broad daylight by a buffeting, chattering, screaming mob, or a fox, with the hysterical baying of hounds in his ears, tying knots of despair in his stomach, or a stag who thought he could run forever, but finally forced to turn, with heaving flanks, and, with lowered head, faced his pursuers.

I faced a stormy sea of frenzied faces that suddenly came to the boil in a monstrous wave that broke over me and swept me through the gates of the girls' playground and into forbidden territory. It was the girls who gave me sanctuary, drove off the overspill of my oppressors and hung me gently over a wash-hand basin.

In a detached way I watched the scarlet stream blend with the rushing tap water to form a streaky, bloody, rainbow that snaked around the white porcelain, wriggling and arching, before disappearing with a gurgling gargle down the plug hole. A girl tipped my head back, she had red hair and rosy cheeks, stuck the toilet door key down my back and, with a hanky she had soaked under the hot tap, tidied up my gory face. Cradling my head in her arms, she made soothing and comforting noises.

I learned something in that moment, that girls had something that boys didn't, a warm feeling of being homely, a 'mother's smell'! I learned something else– whilst in the boys' place they stood up and gazed steadily and self-consciously at the white tiles in front of them, here, the girls sat down and looked thoughtful!

The girl with the red hair walked home with me. I

couldn't find my tongue or the words to thank her so reached out and took her hand. She deemed to understand and we swung arms gaily as we walked along the road. At the gate to my home she gave my hand a gentle squeeze and said,

"See you tomorrow".

Mother had a bowl of hot soup waiting for me but, as I leant over it, a large drop of blood splashed into the lentils. Mother regarded me seriously,

"What has happened?"

"Nothing much," I said, trying to be very off-hand. "I bumped into a door, bruised my face and my nose bled a bit".

I knew I had made a good friend in the red-headed one. She had the temperament to match her hair and the respect of the boys.

I pointed to the soup and the expanding red blob. "It looks like lentil and tomato!"

Mother shed her concern and rocked with laughter and as she quickly replaced my stained soup with a fresh bowl I listened to a soft, familiar song coming from the kitchen. I was old enough to know that everything was right in Mother's world when she sang as she worked. I nibbled my liberally buttered roll and a last scarlet drop plopped into my soup. I looked around, there was no witness so I quickly supped it up!

While schooldays were not the happiest of my life my kilt was gradually accepted and they became more tolerable. Although my kilt didn't make many friends for me the animals and birds didn't seem to mind, and a visit to Edinburgh Zoo was sheer bliss. This always seemed to happen on a morning that the sun rose early and beamed all day.

We started off in the cosy intimate atmosphere of the family car, with light-hearted conversation and the sweet taste of anticipation as we faced the great iron gates that yawned majestically to admit us to this wonderful Wonderland, not a Fairyland or a place that dreams were made of. This was where everything looked and smelt of reality.

It was then that something deep inside seemed to guide me to the giant aviary, to the shrill calls and exotic colours of the tropical birds. I was sure they had been freshly painted before our arrival. I made close friends with a snowy-white, lemon-crested, cockatoo who crowded his feathered body tightly against the netting and in a low, husky, persuasive voice invited me to,

"Scratch a poll".

I knew he couldn't say "Tickle my Tummy", or was too shy to, when this was what he really wanted and showed his appreciation of my understanding by an ecstatic raising and lowering of his delicate crest.

Next to him were the birds of prey, at the end of the line of single cages. I stopped at the vultures residences. The ticket read 'From Africa' and on a perch near the roof the huge bird sat motionless, feathered shoulders hunched to hide his naked, scrawny, neck. He seemed to be dreaming. Was it about gliding leisurely in the burning blue skies, watching in ever increasing circles, searching always searching, for the remains of the lioness' kill or, better still, to spot a beast that had come to the end of its journey and lain down for the last time? It is time for the vulture to make his hop-hoppity landing and remain at a respectable distance from the unfortunate one that awaits the rendezvous with death.

How I gasped at the cool cheek of the rat which made a sudden, almost clockwork appearance from a hole in the back of the cage, only a twitch of his whiskers betraying a touch of nervousness, but was only momentary. He moved swiftly and stole the vulture's ration of meat from right under the bloodrusted beak. I had the feeling that the vulture knew everything that was going on and let the incident pass without the blinking an eyelid. It was a present from one scavenger to another and besides, I was sure the vulture knew there would be another delivery of meat tomorrow and I was also sure the rat knew this, too.

Notices, placed at vantage points, said,

"LIONS WILL BE FED TODAY AT 3 O'CLOCK".

I was piloted to a wooden rail, polished with years of contact with human bodies in its role as safety barrier. I watched, fascinated, as the huge, heavily-maned, lion paced the length of his cage; to me his every padded footfall was a protest against his imprisonment. I watched the flurry of sawdust as he made the turn and brushed his face against the bars to burnish again the scars gained by uncountable hours of pacing and yearning and longing to be free. As it was passing me once more the huge beast paused, its big padded foot still hung in the air. I found myself gazing into his golden, glowing eyes. I had seen him before; he looked exactly like the painting I had seen in Glasgow.

My parents had taken me to a religious Convention there. I had been taken mainly because I could be relied on to sit quietly anywhere or to go to sleep. There were no titles at this meeting, everyone addressed each other as "brother" and "sister" and above, stretching right across the hall, was a huge, colourful banner depicting a lion and a lamb nuzzling and making friends with each other. Underneath, the bold letters spelled,

"When the lion lies down with the lamb, millions now living will never die".

Even the mention of the king of the beasts reminds me of my possible immortality.

The notice at the top of the lion's cage repeated the

message, 'Lions will be fed at 3 p.m.' and the beast in front of me knew it to the second. In his throbbing throat was born a growl that grew in volume to a thunderous roar as it heard the metal wheels of the approaching meat trolley squeal under the weight of its gory load. I watched in horror as the keeper undid the rusty iron latch at the bottom of the cage, stuffed the selection of bloody offerings and raising a weapon, which was a cross between a spear and harpoon, he deftly speared the half of a horse's head. The empty eye socket reflected only death and despair and dispassionately resigned itself to the fierce, clutching, embrace of the lion's claws.

A strange, cold, wind blew over and around me as I gazed again into the lion's eyes and saw only the burning wish that this had been his captor and his captor's bones he was crunching.

I was led away to the sea-lions pool, where the feeding time was 3.30 p.m. I was fitted into a niche in the crooked stone wall surrounding the pool. Leaning over as far as I dare I breathlessly watched the sea-lions as they sped through the murky waters like streamlined torpedoes. There was no need to announce that it was now High Tea time for the sea-lions as a large bucket brought by a perspiring keeper, spoke for itself.

The inmates of the pool had already got the message and brought the water to the boil. The excitement gripped me bodily and I hung precariously over the wall, determined to miss nothing, absolutely nothing. Suddenly the water below me erupted and, in a trance, I watched a monster weave its way upwards towards me and I found myself staring into a fearsome bewhiskered face. In my sharp intake of breath I almost choked over the hot smell of strong fish. Fascinated, I found I still had time to notice the rows of gleaming teeth as the rubbery lips rolled back, and they closed like a trap on my arm.

This was truly a horrific moment as I felt myself about to be dragged down into those murky, slimy, depths in the grip of this monster. Then came glorious relief as the sleeve of my brand new kilt jacket ripped off and my assailant fell back to hit the water with almighty smack!

I was escorted by two keepers to the First Aid Post and, for the first time in my life, a feeling of self importance came over me. It appeared that among a catalogue of injuries inflicted by the animals on visitors, I was the first to have a sea-lion bite and I proudly held out my arm for cauterising, not knowing that a state of shock was preserving my composure.

It was reported a week later, in the newspapers, that a sea-lion, always a restless inmate of the Zoo had escaped and, flapping his way through the city at night, had finally dived into the Water of Leith and thence to the open sea.

I knew then he hadn't really meant to attack me–he only wanted to be free! So, I forgave him and showed off the scars on my arm to anyone who was interested.

By now, it was time for the unforgettable experience of tea at the Big House. It was a building that summoned immediate respect. The aroma of the offerings from the kitchen permanently expanded the nostrils of the gigantic bull moose head that looked down on us, ensuring that our entrance was a dignified one. There was nothing formal about the bunch of spring flowers placed in the centre of our table, they seemed to be having a party.

Primroses, violets and pansies took turns at jostling and cuddling in a friendly fashion, whilst those at the edge of the vase peeked curiously over the table at the tiny pots of succulent jam and the plates stacked with dainty wafer-thin slices of bread and butter. I thought it was a feast fit for a king and was watched, from the opposite wall, by a majestic head with long, tapering, horns that spiralled into vicious points. I had read about him in the information leaflet, learning that he was a 'lion killer' throwing back his head as the lion sprung and spearing him as he landed on the antelope's back.

I had the feeling that all the antelope wanted to do, at that moment, was share the delicious slices of bread and butter and the little pots of jam.

2

With my homework from school I had been given a Catechism to learn by heart for next morning's Bible Class. My father frowned deeply, went to his desk, and wrote a note. When my father took up his pen in this frame of mind I knew it was something of importance to him. He wrote slowly and deliberately, finished with a flourish that signified his signature then rose and put his arm around me.

"Gids", he said, "there is a God in Heaven and his son, Jesus, who he took back to his side after the treatment he received on Earth".

He paused and I raised my eyes to look into his eyes. He spoke again, concisely and with conviction.

"There are no such things as ghosts, holy or otherwise, and I cannot agree with the holy men, who subscribe to the words you have been asked to repeat tomorrow. I will not let you be baptised".

My father's judgement was, for me, beyond question.

The new leather school bag, perched awkwardly on my shoulders creaked nervously as I made my way to school next morning. My father's note and the message it held smouldered in my clenched hand.

The Bible teacher was a lady of uncertain years. I looked at the curls of her hair, tight coils of burnished brown that wove their way to a frosty assignation with the lobes of her ears. She studied the note in the closeted shelter of her lowered eyelids and whispered, so that others would not hear,

"Please stay behind after the lesson. Meantime you

are excused catechisms".

The lesson seemed endless as I listened to the chanting from a seat at the back of the class. As I doodled clouds of seagulls flew further and further away until they were just tiny squiggles in the distance. Looking up I found I was alone with teacher. She was looking straight at me, nervously licking her lips.

"But why?" The question released her eyebrows to spring upwards, setting their black and titian hairs into a struggle for supremacy. I said the only thing I could think of.

"Because", I began uncertainly, then blurted out, "I won't be baptised".

The Bible teacher dropped to her knees and cradled my head in her hands.

"My poor boy". Each word was a sob that almost choked her. "This means there may not be a place in heaven for you".

I knew she really meant this and I felt a spasm of uncertainty about my future as the warm wetness of a teardrop trickled down my brow. This interview with the teacher left me in no doubt about notes and the power of the written word but why, I wondered, was I not to be allowed a place in heaven.

It was too heavy a problem for me and I felt I just could not take this load home–it would have been to question the establishment. So I reserved it for the little, old, lady who had a sweet shop around the corner. She understood everything.

I always studied the window first to view any new, tempting, arrival and also ensure that all the old tried and tested favourites were still there. The crystallized star spangled pastilles, try as they might, just couldn't make friends with the cool, aloof, pink and white sugared almonds. Whipped cream walnuts regally twirled their nutty crowns and, in the corner, draped sensually around a large vase, stuffed to capacity with twisted liquorice sticks, was the old lady's marmalade cat with toasted whiskers and unblinking, green eyes.

As I opened the door the bell at the top went into a hilarious, jangling dance, alerting the sweet shop lady who was there to greet me. Her eyes twinkled under a crown of snow white hair and lit up her rosy cheeks, highlighting the little red lines that wove a pattern to and from across them like a friendly road map. There didn't seem to be a man in her life, just lots and lots of children with their 'Saturday pennies'. She looked at me and, in that glance, assured me that I was the sole object of her attention.

"What will it be today?"

My decision was made immediately when I spotted the Special Offer, a basket full of of bulging paper bags.

I paid my penny and peeked excitedly into the bag, a large chocolate lay on the top. I knew its inside was toffee as it was branded with three dark chocolate rings and I knew, from the practice, that the 'sunburn' on one side could, with the warmth of the finger, be gently rubbed to restore its former colouring. I knew, too, that Mother would accept my gift as if it were a be-ribboned boxful.

I looked around in desperation. This was the moment. We were alone, but not for long. I could see the faces crowded around the window, like goldfish in a bowl, wide-eyed in the agony of indecision, with at least one nose flattened against the glass. The door bell would soon be attacked by another fit of hysterics. I tortured the question out of myself.

"What is being baptised?"

The sweet shop lady leaned across the counter towards me, her right breast nudging the basket of

'Cheap Sweets' to one side, her right arm linking itself securely around a large jar of Edinburgh Rock.

"My dear," she said, "it's when the minister throws holy water over you and says the magic words that will get you a place in Heaven when your time comes".

I felt the door had been slammed in my face.

"What", I stammered, "about the birds and the animals?"

The sweet shop lady pushed her spectacles up her nose (they did so enjoy sliding down again).

"Don't be a silly boy", she said, not unkindly. "There are no birds or animals in Heaven".

I was left with one final question. "Why?"

"Because", she said, weighing her every word over the sweetie scales. "they are not Christians, that's why", and she gave her spectacles a final, agitated push. My audience was at an end as the door bell shrieked a flood warning, and the incoming tide swept me to the back wall of the shop.

The sweet shop lady's judgement had left me plenty to think about and the first thing that came to mind, as I clawed my way through the pushing bodies, was that I was to be forever classed with the birds and the animals. This being the case it was high time that I got to know them better.

I made my way to the main street. The big shop there had a special Easter Show of real, live, chickens in their window. I had studied them, over and over again, on my way to and from school but now that the crowds had dispersed, I pressed my lips against the plate glass; I felt I now had the right to speak to them. I knew their every move, their downy, fragile, spark of life and spoke tenderly and earnestly to the little birds.

"My chickens," I assured them, "will have a real mother to run to when danger threatened or, when they were cold, there would be a warm, comforting breast to cuddle against and a soft, frondy, feathered curtain to peek out of and view the delights and terrors of the outside world, in comparative safety, and not to be beholden to a shiny tin foster mother with stiff, slit, flannel, skirts and an electric bulb for a heart!"

The only living creature in our house, apart from humans, was a goldfish called Montague. I felt sometimes that the name was a mistake. He could pout so prettily and give a magnified, seductive, flutter of an eyelid through the glass of the fish bowl. But, masculine or feminine, there was one thing that Montague would sell his scales for — a gentle featherlike touch. I slipped my hand into the bowl and tickled his tummy until he wriggled his body and wiggled his fins in a frenzied ecstacy. Then I would lift him out and he would lie, limp and damp, and apparently lifeless across the palm of my hand.

It was all a big piece of goldfish "kiddology" on his part. He would lie there, eyes closed dreamily, listening to the rush of water as I changed the water in his bowl. This was the highlight of Montague's day, when he escaped the cramped confines and endless circling of his bowl; here for a few luxurious moments was glorious freedom as he sped up and down the bath, a golden streak of lightning. Montague reminded me that I just had to learn more about the birds and animals — and fish!

My father and mother were deeply involved in building up the family business and I knew they would attend immediately to any serious problem but this, I decided was not desperate and only be taken to Mrs. Reith. She 'did' for us and shared the most intimate and amazing confidences with me; how her husband continually abused his body with bottle after bottle of alcohol and, on occasion , beat her mercilessly. She had a strong sense of the dramatic and would whisper with the hiss of escaping secrecy.

"If you were not a 'young un' I could tell you more".

But she never did and I concluded that life for Mrs. Reith wasn't nearly as black as she sometimes painted it.

She also told me she found a five pound note in 'The Hole i' the Wall'. I wish she had been more explicit and so saved me days of searching all the holes in the walls, the dykes, and the garden surrounds, for a possible fortune. But, alas, I found no money and years later discovered that 'The Hole i' the Wall' was a pub that Mrs. Reith cleaned in the afternoons.

This Saturday morning Mrs. Reith was pressing the pleats of my kilt and was in a pensive mood. This, I knew instinctively was the right time to ask my question.

"How can I learn more about animals and birds?"

Mrs. Reith came slowly out of her reverie, reached automatically for the pocket of her pinny for what she called her bottle of medicine, had a quick and noisy sip, wiped the back of her hand across her mouth and said from the depths of her wisdom,

"You can read now, so you join the library, son".

She always called me 'son' when her medicine was taking effect, but her tone was sincere.

Next morning being a Saturday, I found my way to the library. It was a cold, almost forbidding, building with two, giant, stone pillars supporting the entrance and great, flat, slabs of granite built one upon the other, to lead the way. I pushed with all my strength on the brass bar of the revolving door. Reluctantly, it gave way and allowed me to leave the noise and bustle of the street behind, to enter a world of silence, where every intake of breath was something I could slowly chew on.

I tip-toed towards the desk in front of me. There was a

lady there, with bowed head and dark hair severely swept back to feed a glistening black bun perched just above the nape of her neck. I had the feeling she was never going to look up but keep me standing there indefinitely. So, I stared hard at her head and imagined I was one of the very latest street drills, pointing just above her ear to bore directly in. That did it, she looked up!

"Well", she asked sharply.

"I would like a library ticket please".

"Show me your hands".

Obediently, I spread them out, palms up. Her face was pointed and expressionless but, caught off guard, she softened at the sight of a small boy with pink palms and spotless chubby fingers. Little did she know that I had just come from a morning session with Montague. With a series of stamps she tortured a piece of green cardboard and eventually, almost grudgingly, handed it to me. Then, with the arm of a scarecrow, a bony pointing finger and the hiss of a serpent, she directed me to the Juvenile Section.

It was in a far corner, with row upon row of books. I used the little pair of steps to see the higher shelves, but was still a long way from the top. I had already spotted the one I wanted, though, and pulling it carefully from between the other books, I gazed in wonderment at the cover. Embossed in letters of gold I spelled out the title "All About Poultry and Rabbits", and inside, the frontispiece picture of a golden cockerel with his golden hen and their golden chickens.

Clutching the book tightly I approached the Dragon again. She stamped the page inside and explained, in brittle tones, that I could have the book for a fortnight but for every day thereafter that I kept it I must pay a fine of one penny. I nodded gravely, trying so hard to

conceal my excitement and thumping heart, and murmered,

"Thank you ma'am".

She allowed herself a wintry smile as I picked up my book and headed for the door.

"Boy." It was a high pitched command. I halted and turned slowly round. What was wrong now?

"What's your tartan?" The tones had a new mellowness. I drew myself up to my full height as Mother had taught me to do when asked this question.

"MacDonald, Clanranald, Ma'am".

She pondered a moment then said, almost musically, "It's nice to see the kilt".

I felt dismissed and turned to go, allowing myself a last glance over my shoulder. The librarian was still watching me with eyes that had grown large and dark. Elbows propped up on the desk, oval pale face cupped in her hands she looked wistful, almost good-looking, and suddenly, so human.

The book was a secret shared only with the library lady. I just could not bear to show or talk about it to anyone else in case they would joke or laugh about it.

At night I made a pretence of being tired and went to bed while the daylight still peeped inquiringly through my window.

As I turned to the first pages the book more than fulfilled its early promises. It was crammed with colourful pictures that really brought to life the bronzed richness of the Rhode Island Reds, the golden Buff Orpington with their powder puff bottoms, creamy white Light Sussex wearing their purple and black necklaces; the Houdans with beady, black, eyes peeping through their daintly feathered, parasoles. They all strutted, cackled and pecked their way through the pages leading to the rabbits. Here, there were woolly

Angoras, sleek, black and white, Dutch Beverns in lilac blue, Himalayans with their smoky butterfly noses, and sun-burned brown Havannas, whose colour reminded me of the big cigar my father occasionally indulged in.

At school the teacher had been at great pains to explain the word 'sumptuous' and, as I saw my father lighting up I thought it was an appropriate moment to use it.

"What a sumptuosis cigar", I said, and my father and mother fell about, laughing.

I shrugged my shoulders at the recollection and turned the next page to admire the proportions of a steely-grey Flemish Giant when, with a soft, muffled, clap of wings, reality presented itself and a pigeon landed on the window sill. It studied me with a bold, enquiring eye.

I was entranced. I knew she was a lady, her toilet was complete with every feather pencilled precisely to present perfection. Mrs. Reith always left the window open about six inches at the bottom as she maintained that this gave the fairies a right of way and to grant this brought good luck.

"And besides," she added, "it let's in the Oxo jean."

The pigeon lowered its aristocratic head and peeped in, her purple and crimson throat rippling rhythmically as she spoke,

"Book-a-roo book book-a-roo".

I knew it was a friendly greeting and said politely that I was pleased to meet her, too, and would she call again? She did frequently and always about the same time in the evening, and we met in secret. Her trust in me became implicit and when she allowed me to stroke her breast feathers was a moment that recorded what ecstacy is all about.

I never saw her mate, but I knew he was lurking jealously in the background. I wanted to tell him that his girl was just my friend, but he never came forward and I felt he never forgave my intrusion into his life.

Inexplicably, the feeling came over me that a home was urgently needed and, feverishly, I hunted around and found the answer in a neighbour's garden — a large earthenware flower pot. Any magician would have been proud of the way I made it vanish and reappear in the sheltered corner of my window sill. Then, with a variety of grasses gleaned from the garden and a soft offering of eiderdown, subtly obtained from a leak in the corner of my bed covering. I set to work and delicately wove a nest in the flower pot for my friend, the pigeon. Would it meet with her approval?

I waited one day— two — three, my pigeon still visited the window-sill, but in an offhand way. Had I offended her in my presumptuous and bumbling effort to make her a nest?

I no longer raced home from school. Feeling hurt and rejected I treated the flower pot to an almost cursory glance, but had to look again to discover my wildest dreams come true. There, in the eiderdown, in the nest I had so carefully prepared, lay a pure white egg. The very next day there was another.

My excitement was at fever pitch which affected my school work and earned me a severe reprimand. It mattered not to me. I had important things on my mind and raced all the way home to find my dove serenely regarding me from her nest in the flower pot. No queen ever sat more regally on her throne. In the days to follow we really got to know each other well. Saturday and Sunday were days of sheer bliss when time didn't matter, when I could ensure that my little dove was safe, looked after, and undisturbed.

I counted and recounted my pocket money and convinced myself that pigeon peas took priority over liquorice-all-sorts, and, finally, with the judgement of Solomon in mind, I purchased threepennyworth of pigeon peas and threepennyworth of liquorice-all-sorts. And, during our intimate conversations that ran on endlessly over the heart-stopping period of incubation, I found myself eating the peas and the pigeon experiencing the delights of liquorice-all-sorts.

Then one morning, the sun called everyone extra early, spilling itself in a golden, glittering, cascade over the rooftops, lighting up the chimney pots and the spiralling smoke that told of those who had to make an early start to win their bread for this day. I was awakened by a sharp tap on the window. It was my pigeon, she seemed to beckon me with quick flirts of her head then bowed proudly over the flower pot, and introduced me to her newly hatched babies. Their naked, scrawny, gangling, ugliness held, for me, a beauty all its own.

I was late for school and took the penalty of extra homework without a care. Care had other plans and was waiting for me when I got home. My father was in the living room, that was strange for the time of day.

I raced upstairs and found the flower pot starkly empty. It was a nightmare moment, shared by my father as he stood in my bedroom doorway. With his arm around me he explained, gently, that there had been complaints about pigeons in the district and officials had called with authority to deal with the problem, and destroy all nests in the neighbourhood.

That night in bed I was alone with my loss. The babies had been done away with, but what about her? It was I who had taught her to trust humanity. I who had not been there to defend her and her babies. I who betrayed her into thinking the nesting place was safe and secure. How I longed to hear the soft flap of her wings, to try to explain, to say how sorry I was, but I never saw my dove again.

I had been taught that, no matter how deep the hurt, a boy did not cry, only girls were allowed that privilege. But who was to know in the middle of the night? I was spared a grief-stricken vigil at the window-sill as we moved to a house we had built on a plot of land my father had purchased in the country outside Edinburgh, and on a spot with the happy sounding name of Fairmilehead.

How I loved to wander in the clover studded field at the back of the house and watch the skylarks launch themselves skywards like little, feathered, rockets, their tiny throats throbbing with song long after they had disappeared from sight. They left me only with a distant whisper of their melody. This was where the bumble bee took over, humming his own song, swaying drunkenly as he walked the deep purple-carpeted thistles. I would capture him and a thistle top in my hankie and listen to all his bumble bee swears. When I thought I detected the buzz of soberness I would release him and watch his carefree flight to yet another bunch of thistles and another bout of revelry.

This was where the magic was. I had only to follow the winding burn and listen to her gossip. She babbled about the moorhen's nest and I found it, a meticulously constructed raft, moored to the grassy bank with ropes of watercress tendrils and their lengths miraculously adjusted to take the rise and fall and the light and dark moods of the water and, in the centre, a polished clutch of speckled eggs. I assured the dip-dip-dipetty, agitated waterhen that I would never reveal her secret.

With my shoes strung around my neck by the knotted laces, I waded up the burn, the cool water tug, tugging at my legs as if, in one moment, resenting my intrusion and, in the next, inviting me to come on. A quick scoop of a jam jar and I captured some minnows and watched their tiny rounded mouths, enlarged out of all proportion as they pressed against the glass and presented a silent plea for release.

There was a stickleback there, too, at the bottom of the jar, maintaining a dignified indifference. I addressed him as 'Doctor'. He had such a professional, unflappable manner and distinctive red waistcoat. I carefully returned the minnows to their playground in a quiet sidewater and the 'Doctor' to his surgery under the mottled stone with the discreet, mossy, screen on one side.

From here, the waters grew deeper and with an ever-increasing strength, gripped my legs with clammy hands to push me back and make every step a dragging, leaden, one.

I knew the deep, dark pool that lay ahead. There was a villain there, a multi-coloured monster with rows and rows of needle sharp teeth all set on an inward slant to ensure that, once his victim was seized, there was no chance of escape, no choice but to be conveyed on an endless belt of ivory hooks down the large, insatiable, gullet. The villain liked the good things of life. I knew.

I had seen him on sunny afternoons when the latest victim lay comfortably in his stomach. He would slowly surface in the shallows and wriggle in delight as the sun warmed his back. With a forward footstep I had disturbed a brown trout. It sped forward like an arrow into the big pool. With a sudden backwater fin movement it came to an abrupt stop, sensing danger which lay behind the fortress like stone in the middle.

Which way to go, left or right? I shared the panic of its indecision. It chose right and was wrong. The monster rose from his hiding place, stirred the water with a deadly swirl that ended with a flash of milk white jaws, then a quietness punctuated by a string of scarlet tinged bubbles that rose reluctantly to the surface, to mark the passing of yet another brown trout.

I felt sad and responsible and vowed that, for the villain, there would be a day of reckoning and I would be there, at the deep pool.

3

One morning, at breakfast, my father looked up from his breakfast plate and studied me critically. I knew it must be something important as Father never spoke unless he had something significant to say and so always commanded attention.

"You are now", he said, in measured tones and, with a pause, glanced at my mother.

"Nine", she prompted.

"Nine years old and ready", he underlined the word by repeating it, "ready to shoulder responsibility. To-morrow is Saturday and I wish you to deliver the wage packets to the men. This afternoon I will meet you after school and arrange transport".

He gave me a reassuring smile and, lowering his head, gave undivided attention to the bacon, sausage and egg which lay before him.

After school, as promised, my father was there waiting for me in a brand new Morris car. I felt proud that my dad should call for me thus. We sped to one of the largest cycle shops in Edinburgh, which displayed rows and rows of all the latest machines. The evening sun was having outrageous fun tip-toeing, dazzling and daringly, from one chromium plated handle-bar to another. As I watched it bowed for an encore and, like myself, missed the transaction which had been accomplished, father-like, at lightning speed.

I was piloted towards the selected bicycle and held it in a vice-like grip, fearful that all this was going to end in yet another of my fanciful dreams.

It was, in reality, the smallest bike in the shop and the saddle had to be lowered to zero before my feet hit the pedals, but its black and gold frame was tensed to go and the gleaming handlebars had found hands of their own and reached out to be grasped.

"Right", said my father in the tone he always used to indicate that no problems existed, "take it home".

The fact that I had never ridden a bicycle before had never even arisen. But, carefully, I steered my trophy through the afternoon traffic and the clatter of tram cars. Once clear of the hurly burly I put one tentative foot on the nearside pedal and 'scootered' for the next two miles to reach the Braid Hills. Here there was a small dyke and, with its aid and a sense of great daring, I threw my right leg over the saddle and set off, wibbling and wobbling, weaving a crazy pattern all over the road.

Gradually I gained confidence, taming my wild, reckless, ride. My bicycle was a mustang that had suddenly tired of swerving, rearing and plunging and was now ready to submit to guidance. I stood up on the pedals and allowed the pleats of my kilt to escape and, in so doing, found a more comfortable seat on the saddle. I passed two girls wearing gym slips, striped ties and small, purple hats with upturned brims. They were making their way home from a school for young ladies. Their chanting chorus hit the back of my ears.

"Kiltie, kiltie, cold bum".

So much for young ladies, I thought, and allowed myself a scornful look over my shoulder. They were giggling and waving, so I instantly forgave and waved back. That was a mistake.

I lost control and shot across the road in front of a car that stopped suddenly with a tortured shriek. The driver wound down his window and addressed me in a language I failed to understand. I blushed for both of us and sped on my way, head bent to the wind. It was getting stronger, blowing out of the west and I rose in the saddle to meet its challenge. My breath was coming in short, sharp, gasps when, suddenly, a formidable figure appeared before me with a huge hand upraised to halt my further progress.

"Young man," he spoke severely, and I recognised him as the district doctor, also on his way home. "You have been given a heart to last you a lifetime, but the way you are abusing this wonderful machine at the moment, you're not going to live very long".

I thanked him politely for the advice and pushed my bike until, in the fading light, I could no longer see him and, I hoped, he could not see me. I remounted quickly, remembering something. It was Friday. There would be dumplings for dinner. Mother's dumplings were something to be remembered for ever, plip-plopping in their hot bed of mince or stew; ivory orbs, light as a fairy's footstep and glistening with gravy, something to be savoured, enjoyed, and dreamed of forever afterwards. Every Friday, from deep down inside me, comes the urge to taste, once again, her dumplings.

In the evening I peeped into the study. My mother was there, the desk light burnishing a golden halo round her bowed head, surrounded by books, bank notes, silver coins, gold coins and a wad of buff pay envelopes. Mother was deeply engrossed, building up in packets, my weight of responsibility for tomorrow.

That night I dreamt I was delivering the pay packets. They glowed with golden sovereigns. I knew, I had seen Mother put them in! Someone else knew, too. I was suddenly surrounded by a band of robbers in gym slips, with freckled faces, brimmed hats and pigtails. They snatched my bag from me with its precious load, undid the straps and ruthlessly tore it open. It was full of

Mother's savoury dumplings. I laughed until the bed shook. Then I did a strange thing; I got out of bed, walked straight up the wall, across the ceiling and down the far wall of my bedroom. I awoke with the firm conviction that I would always be able to do this and so never challenged the issue.

Next morning I set off with a satchel loaded with a hundred and five wage packets with the weight of golden sovereigns and responsibility heavy on my back. My bicycle and I were now married and knew each other's every mood and movement.

I had a plan of the south side of Edinburgh, with the streets and house numbers of the jobs where the men were working, clearly marked. At each of my designated stops I was greeted by a variety of humanity; short, tall, lean, fat, hairy and bald. Some looked thoughtful as if with something on their mind, some serious with a real problem ahead, some joked and laughed at, and with, me and at life itself but they all had one thing in common. They all wore white overalls, smelt of paint and tobacco and had the ability to perform a series of acrobatics on steps, planks, and ladders.

The wage packets were named and, I felt, held a confidence, so I discreetly enquired who was who and ensured that they were individually delivered as a personal message. I was rewarded with a "Ta." "Thanks, son, for your trouble", and the threepennies and sixpences jingled in my sporran. When I arrived home I was tired and leg weary but my mission had been accomplished and my father gave me a half crown and my mother gave me a huge plate of steak and kidney pie.

Sunday seemed to me a day that seemed to hold more minutes than hours than any other, a day that time itself seemed to take some time off. I retired to the attic, it was there that time halted and rested for a space. No-one else went here. It took an athletic leap to reach the bottom rung of the miniature ladder hanging from the trap door, a Herculean push to dislodge the door itself and an eighteen inch waist to scramble through.

Here were all my treasures and intimate bits and pieces; the stretched skins of a mole and a mouse, the collection of birds' eggs that Uncle Adam had given me. I really valued them.

Uncle Adam was a real naturalist. He lived at "The Rest" and when I had stayed there for a holiday it was an education in itself. I was taught to skin the mole and the field mouse and how to blow an egg for a collection specimen, preserved for ever with just a tiny hole in its side. Uncle Adam performed near miracles, too, like introducing the pied flycatcher to Scotland by the simple method of sending to the south of England for a setting of eggs, and popping them into a native spotted flycatcher's nest. He taught me, also that some eggs were like human fingerprints, no two were spotted with the same pattern.

After I had inspected and crooned over my treasures I became all practical and counted the threepennies and sixpences. I had also money saved from my allowance for lunch break. That, together with the half crown added up to an important total. Tomorrow, after school, I would be able to make the first, most exciting purchase of my life. I had sacrificed many lunch time school meals to visit the shop, just off Princes Street. Its bold, gold, lettering drew me like a magnet,

"GUNS AND FISHING TACKLE".

I had stared into its windows so many times at the rows of glistening, blue metal, gun barrels, at the cartridges with the brassy, winking, wicked eyes, at the carefree brazen looks of the decoy ducks and pigeons. I had thought them, at first, wooden and artificial until, in time, they seemed to nod to me confidentially in a longstanding acquaintance. The door handle was fashioned in the shape of a leaping salmon. At a touch it lowered its graceful head and admitted me. I faced the salesman across the polished, mahogany counter and leant on it for support.

"Can I help you, sir?".

"I had never been called 'sir' before and it brought the words to my mouth.

"I would like the B.S.A. Airgun in the window, please". My heart was hammering as the salesman took my request seriously and reached into the window, picked up the gun and, with a practised movement, snicked it open, had a quick glance down the barrel then, with the stamp of authority, snapped it shut. He handed it to me, almost reverently, for inspection!

I didn't have to look. I knew its every line, every delicate detail. But now, now I had the feel of it. I knew the price, too, and spilled the threepennies, the sixpences and the half crown onto the warm mahogany counter.

"Would you like it wrapped, sir?" I nodded, he was still talking. "We include a box of ammunition at no extra charge".

Accepting the package I went into reverse whilst my backside discreetly opened the door.

I smuggled my package back home and, with a further acrobatic feat, secreted the air rifle in the attic.

Next day was a sunny Saturday and fitted exactly into my plans. Like an Indian, with my rifle at my side, I flitted ghost-like up the bank of the burn until I lay as a fallen leaf by the side of the big pool. With the gun snuggling into my shoulder, and swearing a deadly partnership, I peeped through the grasses.

The big pike was there in the topmost shallows of the

big pool. His dorsal fin parted the waters in a salute to the sun that was so obliging warming his cold back. I turned on my side and the rifle opened in well oiled silence, swallowing the double flanged bullet. Slowly, I raised myself on my elbow and took careful aim at the point just back from the monster's gills.

Holding my breath, I squeezed the trigger. There was a sharp crack and the surface of the pool came suddenly to the boil. A great fan-like tail appeared to thrash the waters to a frenzied agitation. As suddenly as it had begun, so it died away and the big pike floated with his green and orange tinged belly uppermost, head and tail bowed to the depths surrendering a scarlet tinge to the surrounding water. In the evening sun his green, gold and orange colours faded along with my exhilaration and left me unsure about the killing.

As a salve to my conscience I caught some little trout, assured their bulging eyes, panting gills and pouting mouths that everything would be all right and released them in the big pool, to watch them dart gleefully hither and thither without harm. But, just the same, I hid the rifle behind the water pipes in the attic.

Time passed and the attic remained a place of my own. With the aid of an upturned apple box I could lift the little window and gaze loftily down on the world below, and above, passing in the sky, was a seemingly endless stream of big black crows. I retrieved the rifle from behind the pipes and fired a series of shots at the flying crows without much effect, apart from a sudden croaking and a flapping deviation in their flight path.

I would never shoot at the little birds that made the garden their home and watched the tom-tit as it made an earnest search along the branch of an apple tree; every bud was inspected, right way up and upside down, a tiny supercharged bundle of feathers that made nonsense out of clockwork and electric batteries.

Suddenly, there was a shadow across the sun, the whistle of a cold wind through outstretched pinions, and the tom-tit was snatched by deadly talons. The hawk had made his strike and rose with the tom-tit shrieking its tiny heart out, as it hung in that relentless grip. They were at eye-level, the fleeting moment seemed an eternity. I fired and heard the dull thud of the striking pellet! The hawk, almost lazily, folded its wings and gradually released its victim before plummeting to the ground.

The shaken tom-tit fluttered unsteadily to the safety of a rose bush and another day. But, even in death, the hawk was defiant. His bold, bright, eye stared at me with a question. I could find no answer but dug a hole in the garden and lined it with rose petals as a bed for the hawk. His plumage was immaculate, except for a tiny red spot on his breast. A flick of my finger switched a feather to cover it; his beak, open in protest, I closed gently. I closed my eyes, too, and wished with all my heart that the hawk would fly joyously away. But he didn't and, as I filled in the grave, the rose petals were kept forever fresh by my tears.

I felt that the gun had somehow used me and I left it slumbering behind the attic pipes for nearly a year, by which time a house had been built near us.

A lady lived there, all alone, and spent most of her time gardening and, in the spring, received her reward by being surrounded by a congregation of worshipping flowers. I could see them all from the skylight window, especially the round bed of scarlet tulips in the centre of the lawn. They stirred in response to a breath from the west wind and suddenly seemed to come alive. I could see the stripes daubed on their faces under the scarlet headdresses.

With half closed eyes, I viewed their approach. They were Indians in war paint! I sucked in my breath and snatched my rifle from its resting place and looked again. The red-plumed hordes seemed to be nearer. I fired at the leader who hesitated at the rifle's crack and slowly fell. The others pressed behind and shook their plumes menacingly. My rifle spat defiance continuously and the scarlet heads fell one after the other, until not one was left standing.

I paused for breath, and looked again. The bed in the lawn was a battlefield of broken blooms. I was horrified and passed my hand over my eyes hoping to banish the whole scene as just another daylight dream. But it wasn't, I was facing stark, grim, reality.

For the first time in my life I discovered what deep soul destroying torment was all about. I decided, in a fever of anxiety, that, as no-one knew about the rifle, I could bury it deeply and disclaim all knowledge of the broken blooms or, perhaps, I saw two boys running away! My inmost self reminded me that there were no other boys within miles and that I had better face up to the fact, call and confess.

With the point of a knife I emptied my money box. There was, I knew beforehand, not enough to buy replacement bulbs and, as I stood before the lady's front door, I desperately tried to assure my shaking form that, at least, it would be a gesture. Mustering all my courage I rang the bell. Before I could even think of running away, the door opened noiselessly and my heart sank.

She was much older than I had thought and walked to camouflage a limp. I tried to speak but my mouth dried up.

"Come in. Come in".

They were the bright tones of one who rarely gets a visitor. Then the hairy bombshells burst upon me, the cairn terriers, Ruadh the red one and Bhan, the cream coloured one. I bent to stroke them and they, in turn, licked my bare knees with their warm, wet, tongues. I suddenly found my own tongue.

"The tulips in your garden. I think you had better have a look at them".

We made our way to the garden together and I made prayers in every direction with my eyes closed and hoped that, by some miracle, they would be answered.

"Oh, dear. Oh, dear", the lady murmured.

I bent my head, held my breath and prepared for the blow of the executioner's axe. She was still talking.

"It must have been a freak storm, a whirlwind, perhaps? Or," she paused for a moment searching for the source of this disaster, "a sudden hailstorm?"

My heart lifted. There was a similarity with the deadly hail of bullets.

"Yes, yes", I hastened to agree, "it must have been a hailstorm", but heard a voice inside accuse me of cheating.

Together we gathered the blooms and put them in two large vases, one in the window and one on the table behind an armchair.

"You are such a kind boy". With this sentence I was dubbed a hypocrite "You will stay and have some tea with me".

The silver teapot pointed at me almost accusingly. It had the knowledge that the dear lady prided herself in her baking and her specialities were 'double deckers', feather-like circles of golden pastry with a filling of thick cream that had been whipped and double whipped.

My hostess leaned back luxuriously in her armchair, seemingly at peace with the world. One of the tulips reached down from the vase and nestled against her left ear. Would it tell? All my fears returned a thousandfold

36

and the double deckers weighed heavily in my tummy. But the dear lady was speaking again.

"My dogs, I love them so much, but I cannot give them the exercise they need".

This, I instinctively knew, was the moment to make amends for my crime and I said simply,

"I would like to walk your dogs".

She leaned forward and took my hand, her grip was amazingly strong, and spoke her next words.

"You are such a dear boy".

It was, I thought, a pleasant penance, but the terriers seemed to be charged with unlimited energy and behaved like something in a bottle that had generated enough gas to blow the cork off. They would point their bright eyes and black, moist, noses in my direction and, in unison, bark a short, sharp, challenge.

I took up the challenge immediately, unclipped the leads and ran to outpace the fastest wind, but the dogs were right beside me their bodies floating effortlessly over the ground and their long belly hair totally disguising the fact that little short legs were working more than overtime.

I raced them over the fields, over the hummocks, through the hedges, up to the hills until I could run no more and fell, gasping for breath, between two mole hills. They were newly turned and I could smell the earth that had wished so long for a breath of air and a kiss of the sun. I looked around to see where the dogs were. They were there, all right, watching me. Their hairy bodies rocked with the further search for breath and their pink tongues still lolled, laughingly.

There was only one thing for it, I would take them to the warren. This was a part of the hill dotted with whin bushes, and their close-knit, spiky, armoured flowers provided the rabbits with the sanctuary they needed. I knew the rabbits, they knew me and no longer ran at my approach, but kept on with their eternal nibbling. Occasionally, they paused to rise on their hind legs, criss cross their forepaws briskly, and have a face wash followed by an indolent pull down of one ear after the other to complete the fastidious toilet, watching me all the time.

I knew, or hoped, the rabbits would forgive me, and besides I thought the rabbits really were in need of exercise. They got it. The terriers flew after them in a hurricane of hair and yapping excitement. The rabbits knew when to take things seriously, thumping their hind legs to signal a raid warning and beat a hasty, retreat to the shelter of the whins.

The dogs followed me home as if every padded footfall were their last. I was pleased and hoped that the rabbits would forgive me when they realised no harm had been done.

At the end of the exercise I was invited into the sitting room. It was a warm, comfortable, place of leather padded chairs and a large, log, fire. Whilst the dear lady busied herself in the kitchen I relaxed and listened to the grandfather clock and his intimate tick talk. We were just beginning to understand each other when the dear lady wheeled in a trolley with a finely crocheted cover, shining silver teapot, surrounded by flower-patterned cups and saucers, and a huge plateful of delicious double-deckers.

The next time I called to collect the dear lady's hairy bundles of perpetual motion I found her in the kitchen engaged in one of her favourite occupations, manufacturing mouthwatering mouthfuls. She had a visitor staying for the weekend.

"My niece," she confided. "She's a nurse, and would like to go out with you and the dogs. I have to keep an eye on the oven. Be a dear, and see if she is ready. I've already called her. It's the third door."

I counted to three and knocked gently. I knocked again, louder this time, then cautiously opened the door. The room smelt of freshly cut flowers and the morning sun was glancing slant-eyed through the meeting place of the drawn curtains. Like me, it was studying the hump in the bed with its dark, pillowed, head that looked so like a raven that had found a snug resting place. I hesitated to disturb it and gently prodded the hump with my finger.

In the moments that followed I marvelled at the magic of my touch. The hump suddenly became alive and the blankets floated and spiralled in all directions. The dear lady's niece flew from the folds, swept aside the curtains and, tossing a mane of black hair back over her head, seemed to emulate a storm suddenly clearing to make way for the revealing flood of sunshine that poured through the window. The dear lady's niece threw wide her arms and exclaimed,

"What a beautiful day", and with a sudden swirl around, added, "isn't it auntie?"

For a moment there was a sun saturated silence. I searched desperately for something to say and a voice inside me, that I recognised, repeated, 'Whatever the circumstances, remember your manners'. So I held out my hand and said,

"How do you do, I am pleased to meet you".

The dear lady's niece picked up a blanket, threw it as a cloak around herself, and walked towards me.

"I do very well, thank you, and I am so pleased to meet you".

In her embrace I found warmth, kindness and understanding.

"By the way", she said, still holding me tightly, "have you ever seen a girl without her clothes on before?"

Then I was released and free to run, but I just stood there and shook my head.

"Well", she said, "there has to be a first time for everything. In my job I see naked bodies every day, and you should see some of the shapes and sizes!"

I listened uncertainly, and she continued,

"If you are wondering–I like to sleep that way just in case, by chance, I am suddenly snatched up to Heaven during the night, then I won't have to stand around on some cloud looking ridiculous in my nightgown, while I wait for a wing-fitting."

I joined in the chorus of her infectious chuckle. For me, she completely banished anything that held even a hint of embarrassment and we chatted together as she dressed as if we had known one another all our lives.

"What does your mother call you?"

I looked in the direction of the dressing room mirror from whence the question came.

"Mother calls me Gids", I said.

"O.K. Gids", the mouth paused to receive a well directed stroke of lipstick, closed its lips tightly then, opening them again with a ruby red smile said,

"Please call me Connie. Now, where do we go? Because I like to tank it".

I had the dogs ready with collars and leads and 'tank it' we did. Connie's long legs devoured the ground. I put in at least three steps to her one and the speed of the dogs' little hairy legs was enough to set the grass alight. I managed to put in an extra step every now and again to make it look, as far as I was concerned, no effort as all.

On my direction we left the main road to Lothianburn and took my favourite trail through the rough, tussocky, field that, over the years, had steadfastly refused to yield to the farmer's will. It just went on its own way, did what it wanted, growing the grasses and the flowers and the weeds that it had a fancy for. It also committed the final agricultural sin of having an exciting pond in the middle, creating a world of its own from the shallow edges to its deepest part of in the middle.

This was the farmer's despair and the frogs' paradise. Here, for them, was home where they lived, loved and multiplied. I tugged Connie's arm and pointed to the big, spongy, green bundles of frog spawn cradled carefully by the water's every rise and fall. The frogs croaked contentedly and we moved on into the little wood I called my very own.

Here, the dogs were kept strictly on their leads. We passed the rabbits sitting snugly on their haunches in the long, faded grassy tussocks, a glint from their soft, brown eyes an appreciation for being allowed to remain undisturbed. The pheasants snaked their way ahead of us making almost invisible side turns when the occasion presented itself.

I tried to explain to Connie that all the wild things here knew the hairy little dogs and myself but, most important of all, that we never brought any harm.

The fact that we were now approaching the piggery needed no comment from me. It lay in the hollow of Bowbridge and the smell that hung around and over it was distributed by the wind that toiled, in vain, to dispel the odours that arose from the boiler which contained an unholy stew of rotting left-overs, gleaned from the plate-scrapings of the city's hotels and collected by the Pigman with his horse and cart. The delay from the 'pick-up' to consumption by the pigs was considerable.

The boiler told it all and sent out a message that no-one could ignore. Connie recoiled and reached desperately into her pocket for a handkerchief. But I, being long since immune, gazed down upon the dingy white lime-washed house and the piggery that so grudgingly held hands. The little pigs and their great big bagpipe-swinging mothers wandered from their sties into the house and back out again. The pigman's children wandered, too, and at times it was difficult to tell which was which, but, with close scrutiny it was possible to differentiate, by noticing, that although the little pigs and the little children had pink, chubby, dirty cheeks and pink, chubby mud-bespattered behinds, the children, in the main, wore a rag around their middle and didn't have a curly tail to decorate their bottoms.

The boiler suddenly seemed to tire of sending out the same old black, stinking smoke signals and punctuated the billowing belches with showers of sparks. In the midst of all this were frantic cries for help.

We jumped the small dyke together and raced to the piggery doorway in time to hear the final scream.

"Mither, faither, the boar's broken oot".

At the end of a long, slimy, slippery alleyway a boy, about my own age, was lying and, standing over him, was the biggest, most loathsome, pig I had ever seen— acres of hairy, dirty pork. As we watched the boar seized the boy's arm and shook and worried him like a terrier with a rat that has just bitten him.

I just didn't, at that moment, know what to do. But that problem was quickly solved when Connie picked up a pitchfork and thrust it into my hands with the unspoken message that there was only one thing to do, and left me no option but to do it.

I advanced in a state of total terror with only the two prongs of the fork between myself and the boar which, releasing his hold on the boy's arm, looked at me almost in surprise at receiving this challenge from one so insignificant. He endorsed this by curling up his snout in a vicious snarl to display a fearsome set of yellow tusks, bathed in a steaming foam that slowly spilled over and dripped down through the hairs on his chin. I closed my eyes momentarily and jabbed the fork forward. It jagged the boar's broad brisket and I was rewarded with a high-pitched almost pathetic squeal, as the beast backed uncertainly into its pen.

The boy was on his feet and quickly slammed the door shut. Together we dragged a huge meal chest to jam it more tightly. The boar ranted and roared, but stayed put.

Connie went into action and slipped off the boy's jacket.

"It's not too bad and you're still bleeding. That's good. Where are your parents?"

"Mither's gone the messages and faither's on the swill roond".

"Have you got hot water in the house?"

"No miss, there's just the ootside spigot".

Connie shrugged her shoulders and busied herself cleaning the boy's arm under the rush of cold water from the outside tap.

"Have you any antiseptic?" The boy shook his head. I don't think he knew what the word meant. Rummaging about the house I found, beside the old primus stove, some methylated spirit. Connie splashed it liberally on the open wound. It must have really stung but the boy never uttered a sound. There were no bandages, either, so Connie reached under her dress, gave two swift, tearing, tugs and produced two silky, white, strips of material, with which she swiftly and efficiently bound up the boy's arm.

Two of the smallest children began a series of soggy, muffled, crying which was always referred to at school, as 'blubbing'. They could be twins, I reflected, but I could not tell for sure until they had been 'scrubbed up', and there was another, a little bigger, looking like a boy who thought himself too old to cry. His hands dug deeply into his grimy face, revolving around the hollows of his eyes which, when he paused and glanced around, gave him the appearance of wearing horn-rimmed glasses.

"They're hungry", the boy observed. "The stew in the pot is for their dinner".

Connie lifted the lid and, just as quickly, clamped it back on again. The smell, which we had somehow got used to, had suddenly been reinforced. With my nose pinched between my fingers I braved the pot lid this time. My worst suspicions were fully justified. The stew for 'dinner' was the pick of the city plate scrapings!

There were now two rows of smutty, expectant, faces seated at the long, wooden table and Connie ladled out a steaming bowlful each, muttering to herself, "It can't be bad. They all look so well".

To the sound of a contented slurping we said a casual good-bye. The oldest boy saw us to the door. He looked grave of face much, much older than his years and seemed to be searching desperately for something to say. He bowed his head, scuffed the toe of his boot on the ground, then looked up.

"Fanks", he said.

If the dogs had felt neglected they didn't show it and bounced merrily along beside us.

"My God, I stink", said Connie.

"We could wash in the burn". I was shocked at the forwardness of my suggestion. But Connie brightened up and acclaimed it a good idea! In no time at all we were at the deep pool, the dogs' tongues were lolling out and we were more than a bit puffed, too.

Connie wasted no time, but sat down with a thump and took off her shoes and stockings. I followed her example and together we tip-toed into the water. It had just reached my arms, when I suddenly remembered something. This was just the time of day that the old, grey, heron with the long beard, would be in the far shallows occupying his favourite stance under the trailing green skirts of the weeping willow, waiting, until, with a lightning stab, he would pick up a succulent, silvery, trout or a big, fat, green puddock.

He was there all right but, with our intrusion, rose with an outraged roar of protest, brushed the curtain of willow aside and, almost in our faces, beat desperately to be airborne. The downdraught of his five foot span of wings, aided by the element of surprise, snatched away our foothold. Clutching each other, we tottered and fell, the waters of the deep pool closing over us.

I struggled to regain my footing and stood up, the water breasting my chest and there was Connie sitting with her head just above the water. She looked so young with her black hair floating around and framing her white face in tight teasing ringlets that dripped, and paused, and dripped again like icicles in a thaw.

We hung our clothes over the arms of a friendly rowan tree, and lay, head to head, in the sunshine, talking to each other over our eyebrows. We arrived at a pause and Connie suddenly burst out,

"I have enjoyed myself. It has been a heavenly day".

I closed my eyes and tried desperately to think of something to say, then I opened them again, said nothing and gazed at the blue skies and listened to the larks singing.

Later, as we sat around the dear lady's fire with the trolley, the silver teapot, the best china and the mouth-watering double deckers I felt warm contentment come over me, especially when Connie was telling about the 'to do' with the big boar. Connie saw me to the door and I held out my hand and trotted out the phrase I had been taught to use at partings,

"It was a pleasure to meet you".

She didn't say a word but, bending down, kissed me, full on the mouth and left a warm, most indelible, imprint.

4

My bicycle and I were now performing the Saturday morning wages round automatically and faithfully. My iron steed also conveyed me safely on countless journeys to and from school, until the day dawned with an ominous red blush in the sky as if the rising sun were embarrassed about the part it was to play in lighting up this day.

I set off, as usual, and turned to wave good-bye. The sun was right to have apprehensions, as that day I never reached home. At school we had a special period in which a lesson was read by a visiting professor, with a name and a reputation to go along with it. He told us a story, and he was a good story-teller, painting a picture with his every word, about a girl starting her schooling, only there was something different about her. She was the only black girl in her class! My sympathies were with her immediately and for the position in which she found herself.

I knew exactly how she felt being branded as different and, as in the animal and bird world, something to be attacked and rejected as not natural or normal; like the dusky bird in a hatch of downy, yellow, chickens, destined to be pecked and persuaded, in no uncertain manner, because it just didn't belong.

The dark girl in the professor's class was more fortunate. She proved to be the brainiest, the cleverest and the only member of the class who had a proper command of the English language, and topped the Qualifying Examination.

As I cycled home that night I wondered how she

would have fared starting out in life, wearing a kilt! The black people I had read about were Zulus, fearless warriors who left all the daily chores of life to the women and spent their time hunting lions. Spreading their glistening, black, bodies around the King of Beasts, their circle of human flesh grew closer and closer, a spear-bristling ring, tightening with every bare-footed step forward. Closer, and yet closer. Who, in this human bracelet would have to face the charge of the lion? I was sure it was going to be me.

But it was the evening sun, glancing off the chromium handlebars, that momentarily blinded me and the front wheel of my bicycle slipped into the deep groove of the tram line, and was locked in the grip of the rail and the lion was suddenly transformed into a huge, metallic monster. It was a tramcar hurtling towards me. I pitched into its path as crunching and munching, it came to a halt.

From that moment I watched the world spin over and around me. Lying on my back everyone seemed distorted; the policeman had huge feet, a small pointed helmet and an open note book, its fluttering white pages like doves struggling to be free of the binding. The ring of small, round, faces looking down grew bigger and bigger. One loomed out larger than the rest, tied together with a headscarf, bulging eyes and great, big, rubber lips.

"What a shame," she said, "and him a kiltie".

I remained somehow detached from my body as the faces and voices combined to spin around and around — a record on a turntable that just didn't know when to start or stop or what to play, or say, or sing about. It ended up screaming and whining in a high-pitched monotony, till a white, polished banshee finally deposited me on an unforgiving hard bed and left me in a

strange, lonely, silence.

I turned my head, seeking comfort but the flat, folded, pillow had never heard of the word, and smelt of cold, congealed, rubber! A distant voice seemed to be calling. It came nearer and questioned me. I said the first thing that came into my head.

"The pillow is cold".

The voice was closer now, with a hint of understanding.

"Never mind, you'll soon warm it up. Just take long breaths. Deep, deep breaths".

A multi-coloured mask was descending over my face. I could see every tinted section and its overpowering smell held only menace and sickly suffocation.

"Now, breathe deeply".

I knew immediately that this was a trap to put me to sleep forever, so I held my breath until my lungs were bursting and was rewarded by a gentle punch in the ribs. I gasped a huge intake of breath, inhaled everything the mask had to offer and knew no more.

I awoke in surroundings that could only be compared to the aftermath of a battlefield. There was the moaning and groaning, the crying and the dying and those who were not dying cried the most. I joined the chorus, and choked over a violent upsurge of sickness. Cool fingers supported by brow and a soft, reassuring, voice said,

"Not to worry, it's the chloroform that does it".

I drifted away and awoke again desperately explaining to the Zulu chief that I just couldn't help causing the break in the lion hunting circle.

As I looked around for forgiveness I saw only a long room with rows and rows of beds holding bodies lying prostrate beneath the blankets, humpty-dumpty lumps that seemed to have abandoned any hope of tomorrow. I started to cry and, putting a hand to my head, found it was wound around with bandages and I thought it must look like a football that had acquired a pair of eyes.

I gazed despairingly through the slits and thought it would be a far better thing to have been mauled to death by lions than sit here as a mouldering mummy. I was soon wallowing in a bath of self-pity and my bandages were hard put to soak up the tears.

A voice from the next bed penetrated my misery.

"Scottie," it shouted. "Cheer up, there's mealie pudden for tea".

Scottie? I had never been called that before and 'mealie pudden', I'd never heard of that, either. I turned round and got a slit-eyed view of my comforter. He was a skinny, pale-faced, youth with toasted ginger hair and a cheerful grin.

"I'm Tommy" he said. "The nurse told me you were wearing a kilt when you were brought in and she said it was mealie pudden for tea. And the tram driver has been in, too. Reckoned he only just dropped the 'catcher' in time or you would have been killed. He was in a real state, don't think he had nearly killed anyone before. Oh, the visiting hour is before tea, just about now".

I had barely time to mumble some sort of acknowledgement through the opening that had been left for my mouth, before my mother was cradling my head in her hands. In half sobbing tones she said,

"I had to ask which one was you". Then, haltingly, told me how a policeman had called at the house carrying my schoolbag. On its inside flap I had meticulously printed my name and address.

"It was a terrible shock", she continued, "and your father is away in Glasgow. But the policeman was very kind and said you were being well looked after. He looked so young. Oh, dear, they say when policemen look young you are getting old."

51

As if this were too much, the tears rolled down her cheeks, quickening as she added "The Sister says you have head injuries and severe neck lacerations". Her voice trembled and trailed to a stop. I just had to do or say something. The bandages gave me the excuse to make light of things.

"It's really nothing, Mum. I feel fine. And," I added in my most conspiratorial manner, "there's mealie pudden for tea".

The tears had to leap over Mother's smile as she reached for her hankie, dabbed her eyes and, with a bit of difficulty finding the place, kissed me and said,

"Your father will be home tonight and we'll both come and see you tomorrow".

On her way out she looked back. I waved to let her know I was still watching. I was watching Tommy, too. There was a lady sitting on his bed. She wore a jaunty little purple hat with purple cherries dancing about its side. She had purple lips, too, that spoke in a high pitched tone and giggled incessantly, especially at the moment of parting when Tommy rummaged in her handbag and helped himself to a packet of cigarettes and a box of matches. Together we watched her bottom wiggle its way down the ward. Tommy said, as if in explanation,

"That's my friend". Then, almost wistfully, "She's a tart".

I nodded to be polite, but it didn't make sense to me, the only tarts I knew were made by Torrance's, the baker.

Further discussion was terminated by the arrival of the 'mealie pudden'. It was very good and tasted like an upper class haggis.

In a series of whispered, one-sided conversations Tommy told me how he was born in what was called a 'single end' in the Canongate, that his mother had died of tuberculosis shortly afterwards and that he didn't have a father or, at least, no male who would acknowledge a part in his making. He told me, too, about a side of life I never dreamed existed, about the lousy, sleazy, 'doss' houses in which he had often been forced to sleep. But, lately, he had been lucky and befriended by a motherly tart who let him sleep at the foot of her bed and shared the meals purchased with money she got from men she met in the streets.

"She's a smasher".

I agreed, but didn't say anything. I thought, though, that Nature had tried to make things up to Tommy by granting him an indomitable spirit and merry disposition. I asked, in a quiet moment, what had brought him here.

"Chimney sweeping", he said, "it was my first job. I only lasted a day. I was on a tenement roof in Tollcross. We had six chimneys to sweep and my job was to shout 'who-woo-woo' down each chimney pot until I got an answering 'who-woo-woo' from down below, then I had to lower the big ball and the sweeping brush. Things went wrong right from the start. A young, newly-wed, housewife, on hearing my call coming from her fireplace stuck her head in and yodelled back. When I got down the Boss was trying to pacify and explain things to the distressed housewife. Her room was full of soot and you should have seen her", Tommy chuckled, "just like a darkie! The Boss hissed in my ear 'Get it right this afternoon'. I didn't. I slipped on the slates, fell through a skylight and broke my leg. D'you know what the Boss said to me when I was lying on the stretcher? He was real nice. He said 'Your sacked'!"

The hurt of that moment showed in Tommy's eyes, but he quickly banished it with the back of his hand in a defiant snort.

"See if I care. I've been here a week now. It's great, a lovely soft bed", he stroked the blankets affectionately, "and lovely grub", he patted his tummy and lay back with a contented sigh. His last few words were framed in a sleepy request to 'try on my kilt sometime'.

Next morning Tommy got things wrong as far as hospital law was concerned. He was led back to bed by the Sister. Worse was to follow as the Matron, herself, flowed up the ward in full sail with a packet of cigarettes in one hand and a box of matches in the other. She paused while Tommy was bundled back into bed, then, in a voice which could be used for chipping chunks out of icebergs she said,

"How old are you?"

Tommy wasted no time at all in replying, "The school inspector has stopped chasing me, so I must be fourteen, Miss."

The matron, still smarting under being addressed as 'Miss' said,

"You were caught by Sister smoking in the toilet. Have you anything to say?"

I felt for Tommy at this moment, but he remained unruffled.

"Yes, Ma'am", he said graciously, "what was Sister doing in the 'Gents'?"

At this, everyone retired and the nurses continued their bed-making with a corner of the blanket stuffed in their mouths. The nurse who renewed my head dressing was still giggling and, combing out some of my curls between the bandages said,

"That's so your folks will know which end is up!"

My folks were there all right at the visiting hour. I found my voice and put the question,

"My bicycle?"

My father's upturned eyes answered it and my mother leaned forward and almost whispered,

"The wages are now being delivered by car and you, in future, will travel to and from school in Harper's bus".

It all sounded hard and logical but I knew, within myself, that it was because my father and mother cared.

When they had gone Tommy was at my bedside with a business card in his hand.

"Your Dad's a big shot, isn't he?"

I couldn't manage much in the way of expression through the slits, but inclined my head.

"He asked me if I would like to be a Master Painter and said he would be pleased to take me on as an apprentice".

Later, when only the night nurse's light was burning, Tommy was murmurring, almost deliriously,

"A master painter, a master painter!"

My father never did things by halves. He had asked me, as I lay in my hospital bed, what I would really like and I mumbled through the hot moist bandages that clung around my mouth, 'A puppy'.

It was waiting for me when I got home, a little roan cocker spaniel puppy, with a pedigree longer than her riggly-wiggly body. My shattered world magically reassembled and was complete. Meticulously, I filled in her registration form; no birth certificate ever received greater thought than this. The name of our house 'Artone' was selected immediately as her prefix. Her personal name had to match it, not too grand or too frivolous, but quietly proud. 'Pamela', that was to be her name 'Artone Pamela'.

When she was just eight months old I entered her for the Scottish Gundog Championship Show at Waverley Market, Edinburgh. In big classes, which included the cream of the cocker spaniels from England, Ireland and

Wales, 'Pam' won four firsts and the coveted Challenge Certificate.

It was Pam who introduced me to Irralee. She was a girl who stayed with her mother and sister, during the summer months, in what was something special in the way of caravans, not far from Fairmilehead. I met Irralee one day on the Morton Mains Farm road and, in passing, she knelt down and fondled my spaniel.

"You clever girl", she said, "winning all those prizes. I read about you in 'Our Dogs'."

I knew in that moment that Irralee was unusual, totally different to other girls I had known. She was very forthright, down to earth and had eyes that looked at you with a deadly honesty. She made it quite plain, from the start that I mattered not at all in her way of life and, that on this occasion, the only reason she had stopped was to speak to my dog.

At this time, our only meeting, apart from the dog walking, was at a private swimming pool near Lothianburn, whose owner generously allowed the young people of the district to use it. There weren't many of us, but one day I arrived to find Irralee there. After a short, silent, swimming session she agreed to play a ball game with me, probably because I was the only one there and there wasn't even a dog around! The game resembles volley ball in the water.

Irralee was already endowed with the blessings of womanhood, which her swimsuit seemed hard put to keep in their proper place at the most strenuous moments of this ball game, when she jumped high and threw the ball, two-handed, over the net. On the way down she gracefully lowered her arms and, with hands and fingers extended, halted any attempts at a possible escape whilst, at the same time, shouting gleefully,

"That's another point to me!"

I lost the game, but Irralee was too well brought up to gloat over her win, she just politely thanked me for taking part. We set off for home together. Irralee hadn't bothered to change and still wore her swimsuit; clothes seemed a very secondary consideration in a life that appeared to be dedicated to animals. Her mother was waiting at the Fairmilehead crossroads, a commanding figure in a tartan skirt and cloak. She greeted us as if we both belonged to her, and to me she said,

"You wear the kilt as if you slept in it", and the way she said it made it a compliment of the highest order. Irralee turned to me, saying,

"May I call at your house, sometime?"

I nodded eagerly, she wanted to see me again!

"But Irralee continued, "I want to walk your dog, it would be a shame if she got too fat".

And so we parted at the crossroads.

My schooling, though nearing its end, was affected by my accident, too, and I had no chance of catching up on the months of learning I had lost. But my father waived this into insignificance compared to the plans he had made for me. He pressed into my hand a letter acknowledging my enrolment into the College of Art, and spoke eagerly of the place I was to take in what he loved to call the 'Old Firm'.

But first, I had to start at the beginning and Tommy was there to give me a hand in the art of tea-making for the men. Before and after the tea-making we watched the 'time-served' men at work and, every day, learned something new. But the moment I really savoured was on my first pay day. This time I was the recipient of the little buff envelope. I opened it with awe and thoughtfully fingered the new, crisp, ten shilling note. Tommy stuffed his pay packet into his top pocket and said, expansively,

"Let's go to the pictures tonight. There's a Western on".

That evening found us reclining luxuriously in the circle seats. As the cowboys shot it out with the Indians, Tommy's jaws worked overtime as he automatically posted stick after stick of chewing gum into his mouth.

We crossed Princes Street and stopped under a street lamp outside the 'Rose and Crown'. Here, Tommy donned his most grown-up manner and said,

"Fancy a beer?"

We were men on a night out together so I breathed deeply and let the answer out slowly and casually, "Why not?"

Together we leaned against the brass rail on the door and pushed our way in. We had time only to smell the malt and choke over the smoke when hands, like big bunches of bananas attached to an apron advertising Brown Ale, seized us in a vice-like grip and, in a booming voice, roared out,

"No boys in here!" and we found ourselves unceremoniously hustled into the street.

As we tried to recover our breath and a vestige of pride a young lady followed us. She wore a brief red skirt and a blue satin blouse whose ample contents bobbed and bounced as she stepped towards us.

"Tommy!" she said in shocked tones, "that was a fine to do. You know fine you might have got away with it, but taking in that wee, kiltie laddie — you asked for it".

But Tommy was unabashed.

"Bella", he said, handing her a ten shilling note, "be a sport and get us a carryout. Some wee heavies and a gin for yourself".

"Tommy, you know you are too young to drink", but, so saying, Bella treated him to the sort of look that I yearned to have for myself and disappeared through the revolving door of the 'Rose and Crown'.

"I wonder" said Tommy moodily "if we will ever see her again" and, after about twenty minutes, I began to wonder, too, when Bella suddenly appeared as if propelled by some mysterious force, holding a bulging, clinking, brown paper bag in her arms.

"It's that 'revolting' door", she said. "That guy going in on the other side nearly did me an injury. But", she added, patting the brown bag affectionately, "the carryout is safe. Let's go to my place and have a party".

Bella's 'place' was a dingy room at the top of a well worn flight of steps, with a yellow gas light that just showed a table, two chairs and a bed with a multi-coloured, patchwork, quilt with a longing to tell a multi-coloured, patchwork story.

Bella dumped three cups on the table, kept the cracked one for herself and, with an opener and a flick of the wrist, sent the tops of the 'wee heavies' spinning into the fireplace. She placed a bottle in front of each of us and poured herself a generous gin. It was my first taste of heavy beer and, after the first mouthful or two, I opened my mouth to make some polite conversation, but nothing came out. So I returned to the beer and emerged feeling that a hand had hold of my neck in a vice-like grip and was now engaged in stuffing my head with cotton wool.

Bella had undone the cobwebby scarf around her throat and started to sing. She had a soft, sweet, voice and needed no accompaniment, finishing with a heart-rending, sobbing,

"Be sure it's true when you say, 'I love you',
It's a sin to tell a lie".

She reached up her leg and produced a handkerchief, just in time to stifle a large sniff.

"It's the gin", she said. "It always gets me this way".

Tommy gazed at Bella with his head cupped in his hands. "I love you", he said.

"That's another thing you're not old enough for", snapped Bella. "Give us a song Tommy and cheer us up".

He needed no second invitation and, in an easy gravel-path voice, sang,

"Car-rots, ca-beans and cab-bages,
Cab-bages, ca-beans and car-rots.
The sweetest of flowers that e'er I know,
I love to sit there and watch them grow.
Some people like rhodedendrons, and some forget-
me-nots,
But I'd rather have a nice place full of
Cab-beef, with cab-bages, ca-beans and Car-rots".

Tommy's long drawn out cab-bages, ca-beans and car-rots were winning lines and we applauded mightily. Whilst we were all having another sip the gas mantle took the opportunity to have a hiccup and shatter the silence. I knew, without any prompting, that it was now my turn. I remembered my mother's brother, when he returned from America, was always smiling. He could afford to, his front teeth were filled with gold. He also had a nasal, down-to-earth tone and a ukelele to which I sang the song he taught me.

"I was in the land of Palestine . . . . . ."

I told the story of Samson, right to its climax,

"With cracks and groans the building gave,
'Too late', the people cried.
"That's brought down the house", he said,
And laid him down and died".

My audience applauded wildly because, I suppose, they had never heard a song about a bible story before. In fact, I wondered if they had ever heard a bible story, particularly when Bella said,

"Fancy that fellow Samson having all that strength in his hair and what a shame he got mixed up with a dame like Delilah".

With a sigh, she lifted her cup, drained it and set it down with a decisive 'clunk'.

"Right boys", she said, "that old, blood-sucking, landlord will be round for the rent tomorrow, so I have to do something about it".

She started by unbuttoning her red blouse and, in one movement, took it off and flipped it on the bed; she unfastened her skirt at the side and, as it slumped down round her ankles, stepped out of it and, with her toe, kicked it high in the air to join the blouse. This, I felt, was all part of a demonstration on Bella's part, not to be judged by her standard of living but by her whiter than white underwear.

As she sat down at her dressing table the frilly lace, that traced its way delicately across her bosom, rose and fell like the dreamy crest of a wave. Only half of the mirror glass was in place and the wooden backing of the other half gave the impression of being watched by a person with one eye. But Bella gazed earnestly into this glass eye and dexterously painted her eyelashes with a little brush. Tommy, watching her, gathered all the courage that the 'wee heavies' could give, and broke the silence.

"Bella", he said, "I have a good job now and I love you. Just say you'll marry me".

Bella's lipstick froze on its way to her mouth.

"Tommy, oh Tommy", she cried. "No-one ever said that to me before", and turned round with a gigantic tear in each eye, one paused and sat on a wobbly perch just over her right cheek bone, the other plunged in a frantic race to reach her chin but, once there, it hung seeming to wait for something and, when it caught the glint of the gaslight, let go.

But, for Bella, the stabbing pain of the heartache was only momentary. She brushed angrily at the undecided teardrop with the back of her hand and turned on Tommy.

"You've ruined my make-up. You, you . . . ." words failed her. But Tommy, still under the anaesthetic of the 'wee heavies' took all this as a favourable return in the language of lovemaking, and sprawled back in his chair, beaming.

Bella was again gazing into the one eyed mirror, making repairs to the damage, after which, she opened a drawer and, like a magician, produced a handful of dazzling sequined material. She shimmied sleekily into this glistening sheath of a dress, that settled with a silky sigh on her every contour.

"Follow me, boys" she said, and we followed her down the worn steps and on toward Rose Street. She paused for a moment as a thought came to her mind,

"Where are you staying Tommy?"

"I'm staying with Mrs. MacLeod at Tollcross".

Bella's hand gently straightened Tommy's forelock. "Mrs. MacLeod's all right", she said.

"Yes," replied Tommy, "If you like mince and tatties".

Bella chuckled as she turned away and we watched her high heels tap, tapping over the polished heads of the cobble stones.

Tommy, well accustomed to being 'left' was the first to recover.

"Let's go to the I-ties".

"The — where?" I enquired.

"To the Italian shop. They make the best fish suppers. None can make fish suppers like the I-ties".

The way he said it made me suddenly hungry. The

brilliantly lit restaurant drew us like moths to the flame. A dark olive-skinned man had just dipped a wire basket into the cooker's bubbling fat and pulled out a load of fizzling, crisp, chips. At the other end a lady, equally dark and olive-skinned, attended to the fish.

Deciding to eat in the grand manner, and not to be associated with those who had only come in for a carry-out, its steaming contents eating its way out of yesterday's newspaper, we slid into a high backed cubicle. A waitress hovered over and around us.

"Hallo, Tommy, What will it be?"

I felt a vicious stab of jealousy. Tommy seemed to know all the girls and this one waited upon his every word with pencil and paper poised. Her freckled face was fondled by a cuddling crowd of curls that her snow white cap was battling to control.

"Fish and chips for two, please".

Tommy ran his tongue over his lips as he was ordering, savouring every second. "With hot peas and pickled onions".

It was a banquet to make a king envious. When Tommy had finished his last mouthful, laid his knife and fork on the plate, he suddenly looked very hard at me and, with his voice lowered to exclude everyone but the two of us, said,

"Have you got a girl?"

It was a moment when envy and jealousy set about torturing me mercilessly, and I was sorely tempted to tell Tommy about Connie. But, as I opened my mouth, I closed it again, realising for the first time that there are some things shared between two people, and to talk of them would blemish something beautiful.

So I shook my head.

5

By this time I had learned to laugh at life, and at myself,
chiefly because I had found crying more difficult and
undignified. But there was a drawback. The echo of my
laughter was recognised and people I hardly knew would
say,

"You were there. I heard you laugh".

It also carried a mischievous label and I was to find an
involvement with injustice, such as the week-end that an
aunt stayed with us on their honeymoon. The entire
household was awakened in the early hours of the
morning by a series of blood-curdling shrieks. The bride
had suddenly discovered that the bump disturbing the
well-being of her left-hip was a dead mouse.

At the inquest next morning everyone was soon left in
no doubt that I was the 'number one' suspect. I knew
myself to be completely innocent and felt a deep sense of
outrage, the final humiliation was still to come. My
mother, whom I was so sure would leap to my defence,
put her arm around me and said,

"Oh, Gids, what will I do with you? You are a naughty
boy", and traced a silent message with her fingers on my
back. So I hung my head and took the blame — just for
her.

It happened, too, on the rugby field. I had been asked
by the sports master, who was also the maths teacher, to
play scrum half at an important match. I couldn't refuse
as he had always given me a high mark for my tortuous
attempt to solve a horrific problem, just because I was
one of his 'Rrrugby' boys.

It was a gruelling, body-battering match. The

opposite scrum half, I had been told, was in line for international selection, and he certainly gave me a thumping, bruising time of it with his tackles. I knew his name, the watching crowd, mostly girls, were screaming it,

"Come on, Nigel".

There arose a critical moment in the match, with honours even and a minute to go. His scrum won the ball, but I was round in a flash and launched my body in a despairing flying tackle. I caught, and desperately held on to the tie around his middle. Something had to give. It did, and Nigel's shorts slumped around his ankles. The girls screamed, our full back seized the ball and neatly drop-kicked the winning goal.

In the pavilion I was congratulated on all sides about my subtle de-bagging of the opposite side's star. In vain I tried to explain that it was all accidental. I pulled my jersey over my head and took off my shorts and thought how strange, when I had the chance to be dressed the same as everyone else, that I had lost something, but it came back to me as I buckled on my kilt.

When the team's captain put his hand on my shoulder and said,

"You had a good game", And, as he turned to go, said, almost casually,

"I'm trying out a canoe tomorrow. Would you like to come?"

I opened my mouth to speak, but ended up nodding my head.

"Right", he said, "meet me at Granton Harbour, ten a.m.".

It was a pleasant sunny Sunday morning, with just a hint of mist on the water. The Captain had a bundle of canvas under his arm.

"Where", I enquired, "is the canoe?"

Treating my question as a stupid one, he pointed to his meagre bundle. I had more than a premonition in that moment that something was going to go wrong. This pathetic parcel was hopefully intended to carry the two of us into, what was to become, a perilous journey up the Firth of Forth. I surveyed the entire outfit doubtfully and said, in a voice that I did not recognise as my own,

"You can't be serious!"

But he was a serious sort of chap and had fitted a fragile wooden frame, which was hinged to unfold into a fragile backbone, for this pocket of mildewed canvas. It reminded me of a Pathe News film I had seen showing the type of covering given to a body before burial at sea. I made a last minute protest.

"It can't possibly take more than one!"

"Right enough, it's a single seater. But you're not very big". He had already slipped the contraption into the quiet waters, sheltered by the west breakwater.

I climbed into the narrow cockpit, already overcrowded by the body of the Captain, and settled myself between his legs, with the feeling that I was soon going to join the ranks of the baptised.

In the beginning all went well. There was only one paddle and we decided to take it in turns. But the sun, that morning, was a bride who just couldn't decide whether to give of herself or hide behind her veil, and finally, disappearing to sulk behind the darkest clouds she could find, sending out a seagull with the mournful message that she would not be seen again for quite some time.

It was just at this moment that we received a crunching punch to the belly of the canoe. It was a hidden rock that almost succeeded in ripping our fragile craft wide open.

"We have to head for deeper water", said the Captain and, so we did, sometimes paddling at a furious pace, sometimes with the slower tempo that comes with resting and dreaming . . Mile after mile glided by under our little paddle and, insidiously, creeping over and around us, was a clammy fog blotting out everything but each other. It crept into our mouths and up our noses, enveloping our bodies in a chilly embrace that left us shaking and shivering.

Then came a sound that jarred our every sense, put our bones in deep freeze and allowed only our teeth to chatter. Out of that choking, billowing, fog came again the shrill terrifying wail of a banshee that clawed its way across the waves towards us. It was the siren of a big ship, whose gigantic bows now reared over us. Before we could scuttle to safety, we were cast to the mercy of the waves.

Drowning, I had been assured by one of the painters who had served before the mast in the first World War, was by far the easiest way to pass from this life to the next and certainly, at the time, it appeared to me to be a pleasurable journey with promises of a warm sunshine and the blessings of birdsong that rose to a crescendo in my ears as I was propelled upwards, ever upwards, seeking in a tortured agony for a breath of air.

I surfaced, snorting like a seal who has overspent his time in the depths, and just beside the bobbing head of the Captain. He was a born leader and gargled,

"Follow me".

But I knew that I only had one person to thank for my continued presence in this world, my swimming instructress, Miss Torrance. Behind her back, and in whispers, we called her 'The Torrent'. She had a smooth tongue that darted around her lips before she spoke, but it couldn't match the quick flick of her towel whose stinging kiss left a red mark on the bare backside that had lingered too long in the hot shower, which 'The

Torrent' always insisted we all take before entering 'her' pool.

Her immaculate swimsuit had on the front, an otter which, when she took a breath swelled to gigantic proportions and flashed his white teeth. Having gained everyone's attention she allowed her breath to escape in the soft, low, hiss of a self-satisfied snake which had successfully mesmerised its victim.

"You boys resemble a bundle of skinned rabbits but I" and she glared at each of us in turn "will make otters of you". And she did.

"Kick off your shoes", spluttered the Captain.

I did and wondered how on earth I was going to explain their loss when I got home — if I ever got home. We had a sea-shell there, on the mantlepiece at home and, if you put it to your ear, you could hear the booming roar of the surf. I could hear it now, louder and louder and, behind it, the chatter of ghostly voices.

The Captain was beside me again.

"Keep going", he shouted excitedly. "I can hear people talking".

I lifted my face out of the water. I, too, had heard those voices echoing through the mist and over the waves. We scrambled the last few yards up a rocky foreshore and collapsed on the turf under a row of tall trees which looked down on a pathway that people used for their Sunday afternoon walks.

A young couple, who must have had other things on their minds, stopped, looked down upon us and asked if we were all right. For once, I was ahead of the Captain, who still lay with his finger tips dug deeply into the turf.

"We lost our boat," I tried to explain. "Where are we?"

"Cramond", they answered in unison.

I wrung out the pleats of my kilt. Despite its weight in

the water I had managed to hang on to it, or it had hung on to me. I shook the Captain's shoulder. He awakened as one who has been indulging in forty winks. Slowly we padded our way through the village, for all the world like two patients emerging from the realms of deep anaesthetic, and found ourselves at the entrance to Cramond Inn. The Captain again took command and signed the 'Bona Fide Traveller's' Book.

As we tip-toed in, in stocking-soled feet, they must, indeed, have wondered how we had travelled and how far. The Captain delved into his trouser pocket and produced a sodden ten shilling note, and ordered two half pints of today's 'specialities'. I listened in a trance and thought that, whatever the 'speciality' was, he owed it to me.

It was a brace of sausages, blushing under a deep rich tan, fat and succulent, smothered in onions and a savoury perspiration. Sausages were, for ever after, a symbol in my life; something that was there to compensate for things going wrong; a warm, sizzling, mouth-watering invitation to keep living for the things in life that sounded, smelt, looked and tasted really good and always, always reminded me how good it was to be alive!

The day was on the point of retiring when I got home. I had never seen mother so angry. Gradually she dragged out of me the story behind my dishevelled appearance and my lost shoes. Her mouth trembled as she slumped into a chair and buried her face in her apron, moaning in muffled tones,

"What would I do if you had been drowned?"

I had never seen my mother cry like this, the heaving sobs rocked her body. I put my arm awkwardly around her and every word hurt as I dragged it past the lump in my throat.

"I'm sorry, Mum. I'll never do it again", I said, choking over every word.

The word 'work' for me had now been painted into an entirely different picture. There was a 'new boy' wrestling with the tea drums, whilst I was drawn apart and groomed for the part I had to play in the Old Firm. I was introduced, as a privilege, to the art of 'graining', linked with delicate movements, deploying a variety of steel combs and pots of coloured stain, in a battle to persuade a nondescript piece of wood panelling that it was, after all, rich, warm, mahogany; or transform an everyday white wood door into a solid, sturdy, piece of golden oak. And, with the master's touch, an effective twist of the wrist, to leave a knot hole that had never been there in the first place, and, yet, have the reality, the boldness and the effrontery to tell the world that it had been there all the time.

I was introduced to the art of 'marbling', a secret known only to a chosen few. But first, I had to prove I was a worthy recipient and undergo the selective trial by feathers. The plumes handed to me came from a Rhode Island Red cock. But when I had mastered the art, the flicks and flirts of the feather, misled even the most discerning into thinking that their brand new bathroom was built with the cold, colourful slabs of reality.

Signwriting, like an uncultivated signature, came naturally and when the special jobs were left to me, I knew what importance was all about.

The first opportunity to leave my mark where it really mattered was on one of the Old Firm's biggest jobs involving Edinburgh's newest and most magnificent cinema. I lay on my back for hours and hours of dedication and hard work. Layer after layer of gold leaf, packet after packet of coloured bronze powders, all played their part in making this gigantic ceiling into something that one would never forget. It was the golden masterpiece subtly catching the light of a dying sun and, at the touch of a switch, hundreds of lights gave birth to a galaxy of colour, a soft, misty, blanket of glinting gold gradually fading to a warm orange, to a deep, rich, red and, finally, a breathtaking darkness that heralded the birth of the film.

Before the Grand Opening Night there remained just one last touching-up job. I had to make bolder the features of an enormous cut-out of a German soldier's head. As I dipped my brush to add a glint to his helmet, I, accidentally, kicked the paint pot with my foot and tipped the contents all over the brand new deep pile carpet in the foyer.

Feverishly, I tried to mop up, but all the turpentine and paint-thinners were to no avail so, with desperate artistic abandon, I committed myself to persuading the blue stain into an unwilling marriage with the rich maroon carpet. Gradually and painstakingly my ceremony transformed the colours into, what I sincerely wanted to believe, was a happy-ever-after ending of deep purple.

I attended the Grand Opening Night. The film was 'All Quiet on the Western Front' and I was engulfed in the wave of bodies pouring towards the pay boxes. I presented my Complimentary Ticket and, with a slow deliberation, turned against the pushing, jostling crowd and turned from the East pay box to the West. I hadn't come to see the film, just the thing that kept disturbing my sleep and tying innumerable knots in my stomach.

The manager stood, rubbing his hand, on the very spot that my agony was born and not one, not a living soul, not a single pair of eyes, glanced down at the sole object of my attention — the diluted stain on his accursed carpet. So I, too, found it unworthy of further notice and plunged into the darkness to find out what war on the Western Front was all about.

I was now on the road from apprentice to journeyman and paired, for further experience, with a master painter. He was a big, bluff hail-fellow-well-met, twenty two stone in his overalls, embroidered in blue and yellow with his title 'Big Bill'. Weight was his problem; scaffolding planks groaned and bent under him like willowy wands; ladders literally fell out of step at his approach. His problem was a self-inflicted one. Big Bill just loved to eat. His favourite snack was half a dozen hot mince pies, crisp, golden, short crust pastry containers packed with juicy beef, with a hole in the middle that belched savoury smoke rings when fresh from the oven. Big Bill demolished them noisily and with relish, lapping up with succulent slurps the warm, rich, gravy, even the trickle that tried to escape his lips trapped by a mopping-up tongue.

But, Big Bill's ever increasing dimensions were proving a hazard in any job involving scaffolding. My father felt the need to do something about it and the apprentices were warned that errand running in the lunch hour was definitely out. By the end of the week Big Bill had tired of cheese and corn beef sandwiches and come to the conclusion that, if the pie mountain wouldn't come to him, he would go, himself, to the baker. Go he did, and discovered paradise — the doorway leading down to the bakehouse. He lingered there, inhaling deeply the tantalising smells that drifted up from the ovens in the belly of the building.

Big Bill never reached the doorway of the shop. Intoxicated by the bakehouse fumes he paused for a moment and leaned against the shop window. It surrendered without warning and Big Bill fell through, with a splintering crash, flat on his back in a large tray of butterfly cakes.

My father was called to the scene and I marvelled at his composure. He paid the baker for his broken window and for the twelve dozen damaged cakes. Then, without a word of reproach, he handed Big Bill an Enrolment Card for a physical culture school in Edinburgh's West End, to be attended forthwith in the hourly evening sessions for five days a week over a period of three months.

"Who," I ventured, having reached an age when I realised the frailties of human nature. "Will know that Big Bill has been there?"

My father looked at me appraisingly and presented me with a similar Enrolment Card and permitting himself his first smile over the whole affair said,

"You will".

I never questioned his judgement, but I asked myself, over and over again, "Why, oh why, did I have to be Big Bill's keeper?"

It must have shown in my face as I looked up at my father. He put his arm around me and said,

"I can't look after everything. You do this one for me".

I felt better after that and the very next evening reported with Big Bill at the physical culture gymnasium. Our instructor was an ex-army sergeant-major, with piercing black eyes, a pointed, waxed moustache and a voice that a foghorn wouldn't dare to compete with. This enabled him to reduce any recruit to a shivering jelly that shook at his every word. The perspiration was already flowing from Big Bill and I calculated that, if he was going to lose weight at this rate, one month of the course would see his problem resolved.

I hadn't believed that there really was someone like 'Morgan the Mighty', a character who appeared weekly in a series of pictures of fantastic adventures and trials for strength in a popular comic. Now, I was convinced that our Instructor was surely the man who played the part of Morgan. His body was a huge wedge-shaped mass of muscle that bulged, rippled, and twitched at his slightest movement. His huge hairy arms carried biceps with the dimension of rugby balls that ran down to wrists of wrought iron, huge hands, and his stomach reminded me of a gleaming, steel, wash board. His legs were giant pillars of flesh and bone, built to adequately support his colossal frame.

He gleefully watched our first, pathetic, efforts to follow the exercises that he had so effortlessly demonstrated, and sneered scornfully as we strained to lift the giant weights he had so lightly tossed into the sir. Gradually, I discovered that, along with a lot of other things in life, the first physical culture sessions were the worst and I found myself rising to the challenge. But Big Bill didn't and Morgan gave him no quarter.

I worried constantly about Bill. He had lost a lot of weight, there was no doubt about that. He no longer filled his trousers and the tops flapped about listlessly and hung on desperately to his braces for support. I was anxious, too, about Bill's pallor. His complexion had a greyish tinge and the unsupported flesh lay in folds around his face and neck. Under his eyes hung layers of folded bags as if the lustreless eyes had finally decided it was time to pack up and go.

I knew then that the worst fate of all had befallen Bill. He had just 'given up'. What was I to do? My father had left me with this charge and I felt responsible. I tossed about in sleepless nights until, one morning I had had enough and rose determined to have it out with Morgan and ask him to stop leaning so heavily on Bill.

All day I tried to bolster up my courage and told

myself, over and over again, the story of David and Goliath. A strange calm came over me as Bill and I reported at the gymnasium. But, strangely, the door was closed and the heart-shaped padlock confirmed this. In a weak moment I almost turned away, but turned again, lifted the giant iron knocker and banged it three times. (I always liked to tell myself three was a lucky number).

The door creaked open and revealed a pale face framed in a multi-coloured head scarf. It was the lady who did the cleaning. Her cheekbones danced excitedly as she exclaimed,

"Have you not heard the news?"

It appeared that Morgan had been enjoying his daily round of golf and he always prided himself on completing the round of eighteen holes, then going round again. But, today, he just reached the thirteenth hole for the second time, steadied himself for a moment by holding on to the flag pole before he had dropped down, dead.

"Heart failure", the lady said breathlessly. "The doctor said it was."

We turned to go home.

"Let's walk for a bit", suggested Bill, and set off with a jaunty step, to the nearest fish and chip shop. Written across the window was a message,

"HOT MINCE PIES. TWO PENCE EACH".

Without a word Big Bill pressed a shilling into my hand and, understanding, I went inside and reappeared with a steaming brown, paper, bag containing six savoury pies. Big Bill took the bag and clutched it reverently to his chest. Selecting one, he handed it to me with the air of one bestowing the greatest of favours.

I had barely nibbled the pastry when Big Bill was reaching into the bag for his third. He lifted his head and looked at the sky, a tiny river of gravy trickled slowly

down his chin, but his eyes matched the stars as he said,
"It's a lovely night". I thought so too.

Just when I thought the world was beginning to take
the shape of a pleasurable place to live in, a cruel bitter
wind swept across the land with an icy blast that left no
one untouched. It crept through the crevices of closed
windows and underneath the doors. They called it
'depression' and we, too, felt the cold, fearsome, touch
of its hand.

My father was a man who looked kindly on anyone
and everything — except defeat. And when it was
staring him full in the face he refused to bow the knee.

"This, too, shall pass", he said, with a confidence we
just had to believe in. But it didn't pass and every
Saturday the wage packets went out, and nothing came
back in return. The men stood around in groups, caught
in the sticky, embarrassing web of nothing to do.

But my father steadfastly refused to do the logical
thing and pay off the men and had decided, at whatever
the cost, to keep the Old Firm, that he had so carefully
trained and looked after, together. He refused to give in
and held on and on, to accumulate an outsize overdraft,
and a heavy mortgage on the home. Even the most
personal of valuables, went to pay the men.

It was February 'fill the dyke'. The time of snows, the
hungry time of the year, when thoughts only turned to
survival. But it held an importance for my father.

"It's the eleventh" he said. "It's Gideon's birthday.
The work will come now". And miraculously, it did.
Somehow, and from somewhere, the money started to
flow again. But it was too late. The creditors turned a
deaf ear to my father's impassioned plea for 'more time'
with the result, one Saturday morning, all the hopes,
plans and dreams, for tomorrow were lost along with our
household effects.

The Sheriff's vultures pecked purposefully at the front door and when it was opened to them, burst in arrogantly. I watched, wide-eyed with horror, as they swooped around with their cool, calculating beaks and claws, carving their 'This no longer belongs to you' mark on all the household furnishings. I closed my eyes to hope and pray that some miracle would strike down these invaders of our family fortress. But it didn't happen and my nose started to bleed.

I dabbed it furiously with my handkerchief, only too pleased to pause and exhibit its goriness as proof that I wasn't crying! I made my way to the bathroom but, in the hallway, paused for a moment. There, hanging in an ebony frame, beautifully finished in beaten copper was Jesus Christ and His Disciples partaking of the Last Supper. It had always been part of our home and I knew it to be a family treasure.

Looking quickly to left and to right I lifted it down and hid it in an old rabbit hutch at the top of the garden. I felt that Jesus would understand and a rabbit hutch was not too far removed from a manger.

On my return I found that no one had even missed me and that my nose had stopped bleeding. It was a time for crying, but no time to cry. The vultures, gorged after their feast, wiped their beaks and departed, allowing us a respite of only two weeks. My father knew, as I did, that another place to call home must be found. Exhaustion, a drug that Nature dishes out in liberal doses when required, overtook me.

Later that night, when the darkness was duelling with the dawn my father shook me gently by the shoulders and sat down at my bedside. He waited until my eyes were open and said,

"There is a bungalow on the Queensferry Road. I must put down two hundred pounds. I cannot do this, but" and he gripped my arm to give the blessing of assurance, "I know that you can".

He handed me an envelope, headed and titled with his meticulous handwriting 'The Formula for Super Glazing'. Together with a card bearing the name and address of one of the best known paint and wallpaper firms in Scotland. My father's voice was, in one moment, a plea and, in the next, a command.

'You will go to Glasgow today to the address I have given you and ask for Mr. Saunders. Tell him this formula is his for two hundred pounds".

Reaching into his waistcoat pocket he extracted a neatly folded one pound note. I knew, as he handed it over, it was his last.

The wheels of the train kept repeating their metallic mutterings 'You can do it, you can do it' and, to ensure I was listening would pitch over the points at a junction. This was the early morning businessman's express, Edinburgh to Glasgow in just under one hour. I made my way to the restaurant car where breakfast was being served, but the change from my pound note after the rail ticket allowed only for a cup of Bovril and a water biscuit.

I took a quick look at the man sitting opposite me. In front of him lay a generous plateful of bacon, eggs, sausages, tomatoes and mushrooms. I watched hungrily as it gradually disappeared and the surplus egg was mopped up with a piece of toast. Then with a careless ease, the knife and fork were laid side by side. I was aghast — he had left a sausage! The attendant appeared, as if from nowhere, and whipped the dish away. The water biscuit crumbled in my hand as I restrained myself from blatantly snatching the sausage. It disappeared behind sliding doors and immediately I imagined it being quarrelled over and devoured greedily by the kitchen staff.

Grunting, huffing and hissing from its exertions the train pulled its many tons of metal and humanity into Glasgow Queen Street, sending up great gusts of smoke to mushroom against the huge glass roof, pouring back to bathe the train and everyone else in the steam that the engine had made in the first place. At what appeared to be a given signal the carriage doors snapped open, row upon row, releasing some who resembled freed greyhounds, others who stepped with leisure, with time seemingly on their side, and some who didn't seem to know where they were going and didn't seem to care.

I found a caring policeman, who looked down from a great height at the card I showed him.

"It's in St. Vincent Street, just around the corner. Jings!" he added, "it's not often we see the tartan worn in a Glasgow street."

The building was large and palatial, supported by two marble pillars that framed a Commissionaire standing on the steps, resplendent in full uniform. He lowered his head, scrutinised my card and piloted me through twin doors whose polished brass smirked at my passing, and I was handed over to a young lady, seated at a large typewriter. She peeped over the top.

"You really want to see the boss?" I nodded. Lifting one of her two telephones she gave her message then listened whilst tapping her teeth tunefully with a pencil. She just finished the melody in time to say "Yes, sir", and, replacing the receiver with a decisive 'click', she rose, saying,

"Follow me". It wasn't difficult. The long silk-stockinged legs, tapering into high-heeled shoes tap-tapped their way across the polished oak floor. We came to a sudden stop outside a door bound together with ornate ironwork and adorned with letters of gold spelling out Mr. Saunders.

My escort slid her hands down each side of her body, checked the seams of her stockings were straight and, with a final fastidious pat to her hair, knocked on the door. A voice boomed out, seemingly from outer space, "Come".

She pushed open the door, announced me in high, nervous, tones, and vanished, leaving me in this polished arena that smelt strongly of leather, cigar smoke and big business. At this moment the sun climbed its way over the Glasgow rooftops, sending a blinding flash of light through the window facing me. I blinked stupidly, like an owl suddenly bereft of its comforting cloak of darkness.

I could just discern the outline of large, powerful, shoulders and gradually there appeared before me a man with distinguished features, grey hair and half-rimmed spectacles over which he peered at me, not unkindly, but enquiringly and securely from behind the formidable fortress of his desk.

Without a word I handed over the envelope that I had so safely guarded on my journey. At a single stroke he slit it open with a steel knife, extricated the contents and studied them. After what seemed an eternity he looked upwards and shook his head. All the high hopes I had held for this day took a sudden dive into the pit of my stomach. He wasn't even interested, my journey had been in vain and my Dad's last pound wasted. Mr. Saunders started talking, his voice didn't boom any more but murmured,

"Your father is a man I have always admired". Then he changed his tone into a businesslike clip, "How much?"

I was ready for this moment. "Three hundred". Three, I assured myself was my lucky number. For a full minute there was complete silence, which did nothing for my insides. They were having hysterics. Mr. Saunders reached into a drawer, slapped a cheque book onto his desk, wrote swiftly and signed it with a flourish. He ripped out the cheque and handed it to me. Never taking his eyes off my face he reached into an inner pocket and produced a fat wallet, selected a five pound note and said,

"That should take care of your expenses. You don't talk much, do you?"

I shook my head.

"I like that", he said. "Have a good journey home".

I felt myself gently dismissed and melted out of the door. Even in the streets my feet never seemed to touch the Glasgow pavements. I had the feeling I had only to bounce once or twice to fly home. On my way to the station I was drawn to the brilliant light of a delicatessen window. There, in the centre was an enormous steak and kidney pie with a ticket:

"TODAY'S SPECIAL 5/-".

The lady behind the counter was attentive and when I produced the five pound note, placed the pie on a white cardboard box and bound it with blue tape. On the train, going home, clutching the cardboard box, I made my way to the restaurant car. The morning's bacon, sausage and egg man was there before me, and just about to demolish two crisp brown rolls laced with butter and boiled ham.

"Just a snack", he confided, "before I get home".

The attendant was at my shoulder with an enquiring look. I answered it.

"The same, please".

The man opposite finished first and ordered coffee and a cigar. I got another enquiring look.

"The same, please".

I slipped the cigar carefully into my top pocket and, leaning back in my seat, sipped the coffee. I knew, now, what it felt like to be a millionaire.

The cigar was for my father. He was at the door with his question,

"Did you do it?"

"Yes", I said, handing him the cigar. "I did it".

I had never seen my father look so boyish. He stuck the cigar in his mouth at a jaunty angle and danced my mother round and round. Mother's face, when she opened the box, was a picture of sheer delight. She gave me a quick little kiss and declared,

"It's time it was in the oven".

We were left alone, my father and I. His eyes were like the loch's blue water on a sunny day, sparkling, glistening, brimming over with something to say. His voice trembled only a little.

"I would say that you grew up today".

There was, I knew, no need for an answer, so we both stood there and listened to a wonderful sound. It came from the kitchen, a sound we hadn't heard for a long time — Mother singing.

We moved to our new house on the day appointed. It was sparsely furnished, a bed each, a chair each and one extra in case we had a visitor, a chest of drawers and a table, all purchased for fifty shillings at Lyon and Turnbull's Sales.

My friend, the milkman from Bowbridge Farm, straying a long way from his round, delivered the rabbit hutch. Mother and Father had, fortunately, gone out for a walk around the new neighbourhood.

A little oil painting, which had been bought at the sale for one shilling, hung bravely on the wall, just opposite the front door. It was of a majestic bloodhound, in pensive mood, and a lively little terrier cheekily trying to tease him. It was titled 'Dignity and Impudence'. I took it down with the reverence it was entitled to and, in its place, hung up the 'Last Supper'.

I waited in the gloom, but not for long. The front door opened and the light switch was flicked on, the beaten copper glowed as Leonardo da Vinci's masterpiece sprang to life; the central figure seated serenely with upturned palms, predicted betrayal, the confusion of the others rising to their feet,

"Is it I? Is it I?"

Only Judas Iscariot was seated, clutching the bag of silver, his twitching hand upsetting the dish of salt, scattering its contents over the plate of little fishes.

Mother was crying softly, in a way that left me undisturbed. Father put his arm around her saying,

"It's a blessing on the house".

In my nightly prayer I gave thanks that no questions had been asked and said "Good Night" to 'Dignity and Impudence'.

6

The days that followed were charged with an urgency to rebuild as quickly as possible and, most of all, a means to provide the daily bread. My father, fresh from a meeting with a big London firm, was first with an answer.

He knew all about the new malleable, marble based paint, that could be fashioned to any design, in a given time, before it set. The picture palaces, dancing halls and modern buildings were clamouring for it. He had been engaged to instruct Scottish firms in its use and gleefully brandished a paper in front of us — a three year contract at twenty pounds a week! You had to be at the top of your profession to claim that sort of money.

I felt, that now, I had only myself to fend for and, that night, in the seclusion of my bedroom studied the newspaper I had bought that day. There, in a panel of print that seemed to be a message for me alone, it said, simply, Gamekeeper wanted for Estate in Wigtownshire.

This was the chance to do what I really wanted without hurting anybody's feeling's and, in my application for the situation, I was, I said, (remembering the tulips) an excellent shot, understood and had a good knowledge of wild life and was keen and willing to learn more. Two days later I received a letter, the envelope bore an imposing crest and, inside, a request to go to a Glasgow hotel for an interview.

Glasgow again. It seemed to be a city of decision. I clutched a copy of 'The Field' in one hand and 'Our Dog' in the other, waving them about to try to attract recognition. A tall, distinguished looking, gentleman approached, asked if I was who I was, and introduced himself. I had never shaken hands with an Honourable before.

We sat down at a table and, at the wave of a finger, were served coffee. I watched as a spoonful of chunky amber crystals were thoughtfully stirred into the cup opposite me, then the Honourable picked up a small jug of cream and carefully poured it to form a film on the top of his coffee. He raised the cup to his lips and took a sip, I followed his example. Besides being good to taste the coffee and cream worked wonders with the dryness in my mouth. The interviewer spoke.

"Her Ladyship, my mother", he explained, "selected your letter from numerous applications, because she liked what you wrote and was taken with your handwriting".

Inwardly, I was thankful that this had helped to make up for my total lack of experience. He continued,

"Well. Good show. Will you be able to start next Monday?"

I wasn't too sure how to address the Honourable. I had heard the waiter call him 'Sir', but decided to simply say, "Yes, thank you".

Back home, I broke the news almost casually.

"I've got a job in Wigtownshire".

My mother said, "It's a long way, away but," she brightened up, "better than going abroad".

My father said, "A gamekeeper!" in a tone that suggested I might have done better to march with the Foreign Legion and, added, wistfully, "I had such great hopes for you".

At the railway station we said our good byes. My father was back at his optimistic best. "When the time comes, you'll be back".

Mother held me close. "Promise me you will write every week".

I swallowed hard. "Every week".

The train made the biggest fuss at my departure. It huffed and puffed and hissed great gusts of steam that dripped and glistened over the huge metal muscles of its body then suddenly, in answer to the guard's whistle, it stretched itself and groaned under the burden it had been asked to take. For a moment its wheels spun in a screeching protest then, gaining a grip it made its way with a series of laborious 'woof, woof, woofs' out of the station. As I leaned out of the window to wave goodbye I saw my parents grow smaller and disappear from view as I left them and my home.

I listened to the train for most of the long journey. It was a one sided conversation, ranging from

"What will you do? How will you do it?"

Even when stopping at stations it kept up a series of whispers, delivered in steamy hisses that curled upwards into smoke rings that danced along the edge of the platform, turning into wispy handkerchiefs waving yet another 'goodbye'

"You can do it. You can do it". The wheels of the train had suddenly become friendly and reassuring, only to destroy any semblance of confidence by indulging in a fit of hysterics as they sped over the interlaced points of a junction to take me to a part of the world where my way of life was to be changed completely.

As I left the train it blew me a final word of farewell and I turned around to find a gleaming Rolls Royce and a liveried chauffeur awaiting me.

The chauffeur approached me and inquired hesitantly,

"Are you the new Gamie?"

I couldn't find my voice and nodded. He flicked the tip

of his cap with a forefinger and it settled on the back of his head.

"You could have fooled me. I only ever picked up one fellow with a kilt and he was a 'Toff' from the north. But you are different!"

"Different?" I enquired.

"Yes" he said. "You haven't got bandy legs!"

We laughed together, forming a friendship while he drove us to the Big House.

It was 'big' indeed, Upstairs, Downstairs and My Lady's Chamber. I was taken over, at the door, by a footman in green velvet breeches and waistcoat to match, tightly laced with pleated gold cord. He beckoned me with a gloved hand. I followed him upstairs and into the care of the butler.

He was a most impressive personage. I had never met anyone quite like him. He sailed along the deeply carpeted corridor like a warship that has never known defeat, almost disdainfully taking me in tow. We passed a variety of doors to left and right. They were decorated with oil painted panels.

One said 'Pheasant', the bird depicted was handsome, brilliant in colouring with a white ring around his neck, denoting Chinese ancestry. That room, I decided, was reserved for oriental Princes. The next 'Partridge', the cock bird with the brand of a horse shoe on his breast and crouching close to his mate. This room, I thought must be for married couples. On the right, a 'Cock grouse', red wattled, bold and belligerent, reserved, I was sure, for peppery old colonels. And on the left, a colourful 'Dabchick', that could be nothing else but a bathroom.

There was no mistaking the door facing us as it proudly bore the family crest. The butler, almost reverently, knocked with his knuckles and, unbending yet with an inclination of his head, delivered me, like some sacrifice of a dubious nature to Her Ladyship.

She was seated like a queen on a throne and rose to meet me.

"A kilted keeper", she said. "How nice. I am pleased to meet you", and, reaching out she tugged a long, red cord. As if on the other end of it, a footman appeared, carrying a brand new twelve bore shotgun. She touched the gleaming barrels with the tips of her fingers and thus presented me with my Badge of Office.

"Let's see if it fits", she said in a tone that sparked off a charge of excitement that shook my body. I closed my hand round the gun, slapped the butt smartly into my shoulder and laid my cheek on the walnut stock.

"It looks part of you", she said, laying her hand on my shoulder.

I felt as if I had just been knighted, and the butler passed me almost graciously to the footman who delivered me back to the chauffeur who, in turn, took me to meet the Head Gamekeeper.

He was a man of military bearing who, I found, could be severe, and friendly, but always fair. He had a staff of four and seemed to rejoice in my lack of experience and moulded me to his ways. I was an apt pupil and swiftly gained promotion to his 'First Lieutenant'.

Gamekeeping came naturally to me, I took to it like a duck to water and there was plenty of that as my beat ran for miles along the coast of the Solway and turned inland to cover the west portion of the estate, including four outlying farms.

My new home was a lodge on the seashore, where the poultryman and his wife lived. They were a nice couple and she looked after him, the lodge and myself. She was a wonderful cook and it was one of life's pleasures to come back, after a long day in the open, to one of her savoury meals.

When we got to know each other better, she questioned me about girl friends and, when I finally confessed I didn't have one, she said,

"There are plenty of girls in the Big House; kitchen maids and cooks, housemaids and laundrymaids, parlourmaids and ladies' maids. What are you waiting for?"

She teased me continually, but I got my own back one evening when 'The Missus', as her husband called her, didn't hear the door open as she bent over the girdle in the fireplace. She was a fantastic baker and, when the scones were golden on both sides, she stood them on end for their final toasting. They were mouth-watering to watch being made and delicious buttered hot from the girdle.

I crept silently in and slipped a ferret to run between her feet. Her shrieks tore at my eardrums. The girdle turned upside down and the beautiful, golden, scones turned to charcoal in the fire. The Missus fled from the kitchen and returned, after obviously fortifying herself from the medicine cupboard.

I humbled myself in her presence and tried to explain that Sophie, my ferret, was a lady and harmless. I had trained her specially never to bite and had only used her as a joke.

"That's all very well," she said indignantly, "but suppose I had been fragrant!"

It took me quite a while to work that one out, but she didn't tease me about girls again.

The Head gamekeeper was a man of considerable standing. What he said had to be listened to, even Upstairs. When the lists of guests were drawn up for possible invitation to the big cover shoots, he would draw his pen mercilessly through the name of a highly born young gentleman, because he couldn't shoot straight and might wound or maim the birds the Head had so carefully reared.

I was called, and depended upon, to solve his problems, particularly in the rearing field. Hundreds of pheasant chicks were housed in individual coops, row upon row, each brood with their attendant broody hen, which reminded me of the Nanny in the Big House who crooned and fussed over someone else's children. At dusk they were shut in with a strong front door to each coop to keep them safe from midnight marauders. But there were those who raided in the daylight, too, bringing death and disaster to the nursery.

The Head sent me an urgent message, he had lost twelve pheasant chicks in a single afternoon. Circling the pheasant field I tried to read every sign left on the land. After some time I saw a run through the grass with a broken clover stem hanging over the highway, which disappeared underground into a tunnel, taken over from some industrious mole. I found its exit right in the middle of the field.

It was from here the weasels were making their deadly raids. For them, the pheasant chicks were tasty and easy pickings. There I waited.

With the point of my tongue tracing the roof of my mouth, I mimicked the scream of a hunted, panic-stricken, rabbit, and slipped the safety catch off my gun. The first face appeared expectantly, with a cold, cruel, look and received a direct hit. I removed the body, stood back, and screamed again — six times — six roly poly bodies. They were young ones, but where were Mum and Dad?

They were more wary and I screamed heart rendingly and tempted Mum to come first. She seemed so much smaller than her fat offspring, but still looked deadly in death.

I had to wait for the dog weasel. He had more sense than to come through the smoke-ridden mole run, but crept craftily through the grass to have a cautious look at what was going on. It was his last.

My elation at the defeat of the band of weasels was short-lived. I found the Head reeling under a series of aerial attacks from a flight of sparrow hawks which, in daring low level dives, were snatching the pheasant chicks just as they pleased, gliding in softly and swiftly to carry off their shrieking victims.

I traced the hawks back to a tall, silver spruce tree, two miles away near the Cruggleton cliffs. Although the young were in full flight they were still using the nest as a rendezvous. I called the hawk family in their own language, a high pitched "Kee - kee - kee'. It was an invitation they just couldn't refuse, to join a sumptuous supper of pheasant breast. If they had a fear of gunshot they didn't show it and came one by one.

I came to hate this calculated killing, but my job was to kill the killers and I told myself I was now a policeman in the world of wildlife. But, inside, I was not convinced and found myself wishing that the glow would come back to my victims' eyes and the warmth return to their bodies, but it never did. They just grew stiff and cold.

The sun was having a last look around before settling down for the night when I reported back to the rearing field. The Head was sitting with his back to a tree, sound asleep, cap tilted over his eyes and a pipe, freshly charged with tobacco, clenched in his right hand. I felt complimented that he had confidently left his problems to me. I suddenly felt tired, too.

It had been a long day. There was something else — I hadn't eaten since breakfast, so I made my way back to the Lodge. The Missus had a way of presenting food that had been kept waiting for a long time as if it were freshly cooked. Yes, she was, indeed, a magic meal maker, the Missus.

The foreshore became an important part of my life and so did the song of the sea. In summer, I loved to listen to its singing, surging, approach and the bursts of laughter as it flung itself on the beach, seeming to reach out with a long, splayed, fingers to claim someone or something, then drawing slowly back, clawing at the sand and the gravel with a sucking, soulful sigh.

It was too much. I would throw off my hot clothes, plunge in and offer myself to the waves. They always received me kindly, the lapping waters gently stroking my body. At times, an undercurrent would clutch me just to show its strength to release me again just as quickly. I made friends with the porpoises who visited the bay. I was scared quite a bit, at first, when they surrounded me, diving and surfacing, blowing, grunting and squealing with excitement, especially when they stormed past me, turned smartly with a smack of their tails and, all in line glided towards me.

I could feel the cold slither of their skin touching me with their bodies. It was their way of talking and banished all fear. They wanted to be friends. So I joined in their games and mimicked their language, by blowing a high pitched call on the surface of the water. They loved it and brought the water to the boil with their appreciation. I never forgot them, or the song of the sea.

Every tide brought a variety of objects. Some, it deposited on the shore, others, it took back for delivery another time — all manner of driftwood from a ship's wheel to a herring box; a life belt, lettered *Saucy Sue* set me wondering what had happened to its boat and hoping that this life belt was not the sole survivor of a wreck.

On one tide a porpoise got itself stranded. It looked so much bigger out of the water, just like a small whale and

I was thankful it was a young one as I wrestled mightily to steer it into deep water. I was up to my neck in the water with my arm around its tail, pushing it into the tide, when it took off like a torpedo. The smack from its tail sent me sprawling on my back and, when I surfaced with a splutter, it had gone. I hoped it would tell the rest of the school about its rescuer.

A bottle, with a message in it, sailed in one day. I was disappointed when I unwrapped the note to find the writing was faded and illegible. Now I would never know if it was a cry for help from some far off island or someone having fun on a boating holiday.

I even found a small octopus, its body no bigger than a saucer and rusty red in colour. As I lifted it up two tentacles wound around my wrist and I marvelled at the strength of their grip. I had quite a struggle to remove them but, when we reached a deep pool, I succeeded in persuading the little octopus that we had to part company.

Another time, I thought I had found a fortune in the shape of an old oak chest with brass fittings, half buried in the sand. I dug it out feverishly with my bare hands and, with the blade of my knife, eased out one of the big brass staples holding the padlock chain. With bated breath, I slowly opened the lid. It creaked angrily, as if reluctant to reveal its secrets. Would it be gold, I wondered, or silver or even precious jewels?

I would have a Rolls-Royce, like Her Ladyship's with my own initials in gold on the door.

There were wads of paper on top. I dug down. More paper. This must be protection for something really valuable, maybe a large, uncut diamond, or a huge nugget of gold. I burrowed deeper. More paper and still more until I felt the hard wood at the bottom. Looking closely at the papers, all my dreams faded, blotted out by a treasure chest full of bills and receipts.

I hurled it into the sea, swallowed the large lump of disappointment in my throat and became, once again, a gamekeeper on his beat.

On occasions, when the afternoon promised a full tide, I would take a fishing line and bait with me to catch a big, red, rock cod for The Missus on my way back to the Lodge. I landed a beautiful fish and it lay on docken leaves in the bottom of my gamebag. I then had some fun with a large lobster which kept grabbing my bait but, each time I tried to swing him on to the rocks, he leisurely opened his claws and plopped back into the water. I gave him best and took a look out to sea.

A big, black-backed gull was circling around something in the water. I had no liking for the blackbacks. They were like the hoodie crows, savagely cruel to the weak and the dying. As I slithered down the rock face the gull gave its plaintive cry of being cheated and flew away, but left something behind. I threw off my clothes and raced into the water.

It was a woman. Her long, red hair and green dress rose and fell with the waves and, swimming as fast as I knew how, I reached out, caught an arm and towed her to the shore. The incoming tide carried us both on to the sand and the woman rose and seemed to stand up with the force of the last wave, then fell across me in a clammy, chilling, embrace. One eye was a sightless socket, the other one stared at me with aid of a bead of seaweed.

I was horrified and fought to free myself from her unholy embrace, and ran to leave the awful thing behind me. I knew, in a calmer part of my mind, that there was no urgency as far as the body was concerned and that I would have to notify the police but, right now, I pulled on my clothes and raced away down the path of the

wooded shore track until exhausted, I flopped down on the turf at the foot of a tree.

When I had finished gasping for breath I gazed out to sea. There was a figure coming out of the water. I felt still in the grip of a nightmare, not being sure what was reality and what was being conjured up by fear. But the young lady was real.

She looked very pink and very much alive as she picked up her towel and started drying herself. I waited until she pulled a dress over her head then walked out to meet her. I felt I had to speak to someone. She put a dainty hand to her mouth and said, through tight fingers,

"How long have you been here?"

"Not long", I replied.

She went on, in hurried tones, to tell that she had been coming to the village for the last five years and there had never been anyone else in the bay.

"That", she finished haltingly, "is why I don't bother with a swimsuit".

"I like to swim that way, too, when there's no one about. I have the feeling it renews my body".

"Do you really? I think that's fascinating", she said. "But, are you all right? You look a bit shaky".

We sat down in the sand together with the oyster catchers calling around us. She laid her hand on mine. "What's wrong?"

I told her about my horrifying experiences while she listened, wide-eyed, and I finished with chattering teeth. I felt the warmth of her arm as she slid it round my shoulders, the soft hairs gently tickling the back of my neck.

The things I wanted to talk about I found I could share with the head keeper's wife. She was a motherly woman who solemnly instructed me in the ways of life and of girls, in particular.

"The girls hereabouts are like the birds of the air. There are some", she said, "who are nice, others not so nice and some to beware of".

I nodded my head in approval, feeling sure that would earn me another slice of cake. She suddenly opened the front door, had a quick look outside then, diving into a cupboard, produced a box of a hundred cartridges and pressed them into my hand sighing,

"He never brings anything in".

A large box of cartridges was not something that one can quickly stuff into a sporran and I trembled in case the Head chose this moment to walk in. I need not have worried, the timing of the ammunition transfer was carefully calculated.

I was invited to supper the following evening. The smells from the kitchen told of tender wild duck smothered in their own rich gravy, buttered carrots, brussels sprouts and mounds of creamy mashed potatoes. The Head raised his bushy eyebrows as the steaming plates were set down but did not ask any questions. After the meal, which even the Big House would have been proud of, we lounged about and listened to the Head's wife's records, her favourite being,

'I'll change your world to roses,

I'll make your life a dream'.

She sat under the lamplight and beamed ecstatically, her husband settled himself in the big chair by the fire, having long since given up figuring out where the main ingredients of tonight's feast had come from, puffing at his pipe and burping contentedly. We were to develop a great understanding, the Head's wife and I.

Further promotion came my way when I was appointed to accompany Her Ladyship's son when he was invited to neighbouring shoots. On these occasions I was expected (so the Head Keeper told me anxiously) to wear a livery, tailor made, and consisting of knickerbockers that strapped just below my knee in the same way I wound my 'flashes' around my kilt stockings. The jacket was matching in a black and white check, which Her Ladyship liked to call 'her tartan'.

After a struggle I donned the knickerbockers and found them more than a bit hampering in the movement of my legs but, when it came to walking through a field of turnips or giant kale after rain, the knickerbockers came out best. A soaking, swinging, kilt always sawed mercilessly when it was drying and played havoc on and behind the knees. But, that apart, it always felt good to get back to the freedom that only a kilt can give.

When called upon, I reported first thing in the morning to the Big House, so did the chauffeur with the sparkling Rolls-Royce. While we were waiting (I always found waiting a tedious occupation), I would wander upstairs to enquire if someone was ready to go somewhere. The Breakfast Room was empty, but I lingered over the gigantic sideboard with its load of silver tureens.

As I gently lifted the lids of one after another a curtain of curling steam rose leisurely and disclosed the contents; kippers, grilled or fried, orderly beds of succulent bacon, liver reclining in thick, onion gravy, rows of suntanned sausages, stacks of crisp, fried bread surrounded by mushrooms and tomatoes, eggs in four different dishes — boiled, fried, poached and scrambled. My plate of porridge lay like an ever so lonely poultice in my tummy and, as I took my seat beside the chauffeur, I reflected on humanity's vastly. different ways of life.

Where did all this affluence come from? I must have spoken my query aloud. The chauffeur, eyes firmly fixed

on the road ahead, gave the answer with pursed lips. He half whistled one, single, word,
   "Whisky".

7

My 'beat' with its four large farms, Cruggleton, Boreland, Cults and Palmallet, were, when the time came, the first to be shot over. Then, the lives of the partridges, pheasants and hares were to be put at deadly risk. I had watched over and protected them since nesting time and, in the acres and acres of farmland, it would have to be a cunningly concealed nest that I didn't know about.

The partridges were the most secretive, usually in the centre of a large tussock, the eggs were always covered with a carefully woven blanket of grass.

It was while checking one that I received a sharp, burning, bite on my hand from a large, male adder that had been lying in the nest. He slid over my arm, jumped into the air, seeming to stand on his tail and, as if trying to frighten me further, flicked out his tongue and disappeared. My right hand had two puncture holes between thumb and forefinger.

I had been warned about the danger of adder bites and drew the blade of my knife across from one little hole to the other, reflecting morosely as I sucked and sucked at the bridge of skin that I had also been told that a cut here could cause lockjaw. I wasn't feeling too happy as I trudged the seemingly endless miles back to the Lodge, sucking continuously at the wound in my hand.

Despite sucking, my hand puffed up into a knuckleless mass. The Missus took one look at me and 'phoned' the Big House. The chauffeur swept up in the big car, shook his head, took off his hat as though I were already dead, and drove at breakneck speed to the doctor.

THE KILT FOR KEEPS

The doctor was chewing parsley, I could tell by the green flecks on his teeth. The people of the village whispered that he did this to banish the smell of drink from his breath. As he gave me a 'jag' and dressed my hand he told me about his last case of adder bite — a farmer's wife who got bitten while collecting peats and, in her panic, kept running and running.

"Stupid woman", he concluded, "the poison ran right through her system".

With a sudden feeling of faintness I slumped in a chair. The doctor took a close look at me, spat out his parsley, and poured two large whiskies, pressing one into my hand. He raised his own glass.

"This", he said, "is a sure cure for snake bite".

I had pheasants, too, of the wild variety, born and bred in the fields and hedgerows. And, sometimes, a hand-reared brood would decide to emigrate and fly over the big wall that surrounded the estate. One such was a Melanistic hen, with dark chestnut coloured plumage, delicately edged with black, with a touch of emerald green on her neck. She had a bold, bright, eye that looked straight at you from underneath a scarlet wattle. It always looked to me as if she had been using lipstick on her eyebrows.

This hen had been brought as an egg in a special batch to introduce a number of beautiful black pheasants to the estate. She had been hatched and reared by the Head but she decided, after experiencing the first 'cover' shoot that the wild outside was the healthier place to be. By the time I found her in the wilds she had already selected a mate and was sitting on eggs. She had chosen a secluded spot for her nest, beside an old, mossy, dyke and under a fern that drooped to cover her, all but that beady eye.

Every day, in the passing, I said,

"Hello. Are you all right?"

The glint that came from her eye was full of confidence that I was a friend, and the day dawned when she really needed one.

She was still sitting under the fern, but it was spattered with blood and I could see that some of her flight feathers were missing. The eye was no longer bold but still looked straight at me, in a plea for help. I was on my way home, tired and hungry, but I sat down by her side. We would see this out together.

The evening was casting shadows, seeing how far it could throw them, when, the peace was broken by sounds of snuffling, snorting and squealing, and two large hedgehogs suddenly appeared. They were after the eggs. One, I was sure, had tried before and had been beaten back by the gallant hen, but he had now brought reinforcements. I killed them both, quite dispassionately. They were sneak thieves, robbers, who were quite capable of killing, too.

Two days later, the nest contained only broken shells, with the message that the pheasant was somewhere near with twelve chicks. Hen pheasants are normally not the best of mothers. This one was to prove the exception. She never lost a chick; if one was stuck 'peep, peep, peeping' in a deep ditch she would rush back to collect it, patiently waiting with encouraging 'clucks' until it made a supreme effort, clambered out and joined the rest of the brood.

It was the first of October and I had a message from the Head.

"There are guests at the Big House would like a 'dust' at the partridges and, of course, a wild pheasant or two".

We walked all the stubble fields where the birds were feeding on the left-over grains of oats and wheat. They flew to the corner of a turnip field, which was already packed with game including, I knew, the Melanistic hen and her beautiful black family.

The shooting line moved forward mercilessly and the partridge rose and fell.

The 'guns', I moaned to myself, had been carefully chosen for this day. Then the pheasants started to rise, and fall, too, I counted nine and could stand it no longer. I blew my whistle and, magically, everything stopped.

The Honourable left his position on the left flank and stalked towards me. He looked so tall as he towered over me, with eyebrows raised, asking for an explanation.

"The hen", I said "and her last three. We need them for stock".

He never questioned my authority but, in a loud clear voice, said,

"Pass the message. No shooting until the next whistle".

I waved the line forward. Two young hens rose together, the picture of their mother, then a velvety black cock, trimmed with green and gold, (he had not donned his adult plumage yet) and, last of all, the hen herself. Her flight was unhurried and majestic. I tried to tell myself that she glanced over her wing at her protector.

When they were all just dots in the sky, I blew my whistle again.

Poachers were a cunning race, for which we had to keep a constant lookout. Not the farm hands, who took the occasional rabbit, or bird, for the pot, but the 'professionals' who traded their ill-gotten gains for hard cash.

I was never really troubled on my beat, being mostly open farmland and sea coast where a poacher could be spotted from miles away. But I ensured good relations with the farm workers by regularly knocking at their cottage doors and handing in a pair of rabbits. The Head knew, and approved, but he did not know about the cock pheasant I slipped into each house at Christmas, and a brace where there was a family.

One day I stopped at a cottage near the estate big wall. I had a pair of woodpigeons as a present for the lady who lived there and who never failed to come rushing out with a cup of tea when I passed by. She was the woodman's wife who loved a 'wee blether', as she called it, to break the loneliness of the day. She was from The City and missed the sound of the passing foot. There was no sign of her today.

I tapped at the door. She eventually appeared looking flushed, harassed and not a little worried. Little particles of down floated through the air around her. Wordlessly, I handed over the pigeons to her when she started to cry silently and, between the sobs, confessed she had been plucking pheasant.

"Bill killed it with a stone when he was working in the woods yesterday". She gripped my arm tightly. "You won't tell? He'd get the sack".

"No", I said. "I won't tell just so long as he doesn't make a habit of it. And, anyway," I added, "It wasn't a hen".

The woodman's wife dabbed her eyes with the corner of her apron and, with a shuddering sigh, asked,

"How did you know it was a cock pheasant?"

"You," I gently told her, "were wearing one of his breast feathers in your hair".

We both laughed together, she with a sense of relief and I, with the feeling that the passing cup of tea would remain a pleasureable part of my day on the Cruggleton beat.

It was the hundreds of hand reared birds, roosting in the estate larch trees, that attracted the professionals and, before the big cover shoots, it meant continual night watching, especially when there was a full moon. I didn't care much for this watching. It was a spooky experience and when the night frost came down and caught me napping, as it sometimes did, it would cover me with a glistening cloak and the chill seeped through to my bones. But the Head seemed to revel in it as we settled down among the larches. They had already dropped their needles and left the pheasants roosting on their naked limbs. Bathed in the bright moonlight to make them a perfect target.

The Head started off by telling me how the poachers used to be dealt with.

"Mantraps", he said, clicking his teeth in satisfaction. "Traps with steel, big steel, jaws that could break a man's leg, set carefully in the pathways to the covers. Then they (referring to the law makers) made them illegal".

He spat out his disgust. Poachers, to the Head, were the lowest form of animal life. He was, I knew, also yearning for a pipeful of his favourite tobacco but that was taboo tonight; the flare of a match and the scent of tobacco smoke lingering around on the night air would be enough to warn sensitive nostrils. So he turned his attention to me.

"Laddie, you just don't put the kilt on, you wear it as part of yourself".

I knew what was coming — war stories. They were frowned upon by his wife but here, in the silence of the moonlit covers, he could indulge himself. He suddenly straightened as though a ramrod had been thrust up his back.

"I was in a kilted regiment during the war. The 'Top Brass' said, 'Give me a soldier in a kilt and I have a man and a half' and", he threw his chest out farther, "we really frightened the enemy. They called us 'The ladies

106

from Hell'.''

I nodded and nodded and dropped off in the middle of the Battle of the Somme, only to be rudely awakened by a stabbing poke in my side. I thought I had been bayoneted, but it was only the Head's finger.

"There's shots in the top wood", he hissed.

My duffle coat was white with frost as I rose, shivering, to follow him. I now heard the shots, too. They were close and we both dropped to the ground and crawled forward, as stealthy as any night patrol. A shot crashed just over my head. I saw the flame from the gun muzzle and the sharp smell of cordite filled my nostrils. I saw something else, a shadowy figure almost on top of me.

In a rugby tackle I dived at his legs. He fell, striking his head on the trunk of a larch tree and lay groaning, fearsomely. Turning around, I saw a man sitting astride the Head, by all appearances, intent on throttling him. My foot kicked something. It was a sawn-off shot gun. I picked it up by the barrels, swung it in a half circle and hit the Head's assailant with the butt, right in the centre of his cloth cap. He collapsed without a sound.

"Well," said the Head, as he rose gasping for breath, "we got these two beauties, but, first, we'll pick up the evidence and then get their names and numbers."

I hated to remind the Head that the war was over and people just didn't have numbers any more, but we got busy and gathered up the dead pheasants. By the time we had picked up the last, the poachers had vanished!

I felt relieved and, I'm sure, the Head, for all his outward show of frustration, was too.

The Head never frequented the 'Galloway Arms'.

"It doesn't pay", he said, brushing his moustache, "to let them know where you are".

But the following night, before reporting for duty I

slipped down to the village and into the bar. They were there all right; one with a huge, purple, bruise on his temple and the other balancing a cloth cap on the bandage around his head.

Casually, I passed the time of day, inquired and commiserated upon their injuries.

"Sure", one said, with an accent as thick as Irish stew, "we ran into a bit of heavy weather last night".

The landlord slapped the counter with a hearty,

"Well, well. If it isn't the young gamie!"

There was an immediate stiffening of the atmosphere but I pretended not to notice and, although there were only three of us in the bar, grandly ordered "Drinks all round".

From underneath the edge of his bandage the biggest one squinted at me with a bloodshot eye and raised his foaming pint tumbler,

"You good health, surr".

Later, as we settled down in the moonlight I gave the news to the Head.

"They were seamen. Incomers, Irish, I think and both with very sore heads".

The Head allowed himself a deep chuckle, fingered his pipe, but settled for a piece of tobacco which he popped into his mouth and shifted into a nest in his cheek.

We were advancing up Hill 60 in the face of heavy shell fire, when I dropped off to sleep, once again.

It was time for the woodcock to leave Scandinavia and escape the severe winter there, winding their way across the North Sea, seeking the comparative softness of our climate, and a way of life that would suit their long, soft-billed feeding habits.

They were Her Ladyship's favourite dish, gently roasted and served up on a bed of crisp, golden, fried bread.

There was a telephone call from the old keeper that the woodcock were 'in' on the Kirkcowan Moors. The grouse shoot on the higher land was kept to make the twelfth of August a glorious occasion, but mainly for the salmon fishing in the river there and the old keeper was the man who knew all about salmon. He looked after the Gentry, as he called them, who wished to catch a big fish.

In his time he had catered to a long list of nobility, and personalities, too. One of his idols was Sir Harry Lauder and he proudly showed me the gold watch that 'Harry' had personally presented him with.

On our walk over the moor he showed me other things, too; how to pick up an adder as it lay basking in the sun on a sheep track. The secret he shared with me — a quick swoop to catch the snake just behind the head, between the finger and thumb. I held up a copper coloured female, writhing impotently, and gained a nod of approval.

The old keeper showed me something more — flowers posing as innocent daisies, which waited for a fat fly to land on their sticky bosoms. Their victims' struggles caused the tentacles to close relentlessly to devour its meal.

"They're Carney Voras, these flowers", the old keeper told me.

He had also heard of my saving the black melanistic hen and the last of her brood.

"That was good thinking", he said, "to look after them Minilastics".

The Old keeper was a good fisherman and could cast a long, true, line to land right in front of a fish's nose. He was also a good shot and quick on the trigger. I had heard of his reputation and was keen to find out who would be quickest on the draw. I didn't have long to wait. My little, red roan spaniel was busy quartering the ground and, though some gundogs will refuse to retrieve a woodcock, Rusty was a cocker and bred for just this job. He inspected every tuft of heather, clump of bracken and wild briar bush and any occupant was the subject of a hasty eviction.

Rusty flushed the first bird between us. Both our guns spoke as one and I realised I would have to be quicker to claim a bird of my own. If you wish to shoot a woodcock you have to be very quick before it starts to take that zig-zagging evasive flight for which it is famous. In no time as all we had three brace.

"That's enough", I said, then remembering the Head's wife, added "we'll, just take another two".

The old keeper showed me then how the woodcock carries an artist's brush in each wing, in the tiny, beautifully tapered, pin feathers.

Making our way back we had to clamber through a roadside fence. I went first and the keeper followed. His gun was, like himself, nicely old-fashioned and, as he pulled it after him, one of the trigger hammers caught in a strand of wire, was drawn back and then released. Just as I turned to speak I faced the shock of the explosion, choked on the cloud of cordite and felt a burning pain in my hand.

The old keeper lay on the ground clutching his arm just where the gun had blown his bicep away and the blood spurted upwards in a gory fountain. I quickly put a tourniquet around what was left of his arm with a rabbit snare from my gamebag. He was still conscious so I slipped his other arm around my neck and, together, we stumbled the last half mile to the waiting car.

"Where's the nearest hospital?" I shouted to the chauffeur.

"Stranraer".

"Right. Drive as fast as you can".

We were approaching an Inn on the outskirts of Stranraer and the old keeper had spotted it.

"Can we not stop for just one?", he pleaded.

He loved his dram, but I had been told that spirits and bleeding did not go together, and shook my head. I studied the thick blobs of scarlet blood that dripped from the blood soaked sleeve and marvelled that it didn't have the golden tint of whisky. It was only thoughts like these that kept me from being violently sick, also the fact that I was frantically worried about the old keeper's loss of blood and I turned again the trigger pin of my snare tourniquet to lessen the flow.

We got him to the Stranraer hospital where they performed the miracle of saving his mutilated arm, but his days of being 'quick on the trigger' were over. He would never lift a gun again.

I borrowed a motor byke and went to visit him next day. He was sitting up in bed and, with the aid of his good arm, studying the newspaper.

"You made the front page," I said.

"Aye", grunted the old keeper, "and they say I'm sixty five. Man, I'm much younger than that. I won't be sixty five for another month!" He looked quickly around. "You wouldn't happen to have 'a drop' with you?"

It was such a relief to laugh again and, when I happen to look at the pellet still embedded in the palm of my right hand, I think of the old keeper.

I had to fill in for a fishing expedition for the simple reason that no one else would take it on, and what I didn't know about salmon fishing would have filled a book. I got a last comforting word from the Head keeper,

"Look well after her, she's Royalty".

I was prepared for someone wearing purple robes and a crown, not a slip of a girl, who chattered incessantly and enthusiastically about the object of her visit — to catch her first salmon.

After a short pause she said wistfully, "I suppose you have caught lots of salmon".

I, too, had still to catch my first, but shrugged my shoulders as if it were too much trouble to count. I knew of the old keeper's favourite pool and set up her rod there, trying on a cast with a large Jock Scott Fly. I was quite pleased with the way I was coping so far, until the lassie started casting. I thought, then, she would have been better with a lassoo!

Two hours went by and, by this time, the pool had been well and truly thrashed when, in the shallows, I spotted a fish leaping out of the water and generally besporting itself. Taking the young lady to the spot I helped her to pilot the Jock Scott in the direction of the fish's last dive. The waters erupted, the reel screamed and the young lady nearly had hysterics, but soon the fish was flapping on the bank before us.

It wasn't the best salmon I had seen, not very big, reddish and on the lean side — but it was a fish! And the royal blooded one was ecstatic. I basked in her praise and already had myself in the next Honours List.

Back at the Big House it was the handyman who broke the horrible news to me.

"It's a bluidy kelt", he said. "It spawned a while ago. It's spent and its flesh barely fit for a man or beast" and, so saying, literally washed his hands of the whole affair. In desperation, I cleaned and prepared the fish myself and took it to the kitchen.

The cook was on holiday and I was sure that Helen, second-in-command and a local girl, would be more understanding.

"Oh, it's the young Gamie", she said. "Her Highness has just been on the telephone. She would like her salmon served as the fish course for dinner tonight. What's that you've got?"

"It's the s-salmon", I stuttered.

"Looks more like a tartan trout", she tittered.

I didn't feel in the mood for joking. "Helen", I said, "You're good at sauces, aren't you?"

"The best", she replied, with utter confidence.

"Would you like a brace of wild duck to take home at the weekend?"

"Oh, yes", she said, and added with suspicion, "what do I have to do?"

"Just fix one of your best pink sauces for this", and I laid my pathetic offering on the table. Helen sighed and thought about my bribe for a moment.

"All right. I'll see what I can do".

I hovered around in the kitchen after dinner, fearing the worst. I got the news from Helen, straight off the hot plate, so to speak. The butler had reported that the royal visitor was delighted over the fish course and Her Ladyship had raised an eyebrow but eaten it without comment. Everyone else took their cue from her.

So the incident passed peacefully and saucy Helen got her brace of wild duck.

Gamekeeping was a seven day occupation, but, if it was something important, I asked for, and got, a day off. I went to Newton Stewart with something on my mind. I was looking for a present for the Head's wife. I felt I owed her so much for all her kindness and it had to be something special.

I saw it, in a jeweller's window. It was a string of amber beads. I knew their origin, pieces of fossilised pine resin washed up on the beaches, then collected, cut and polished. They were beautiful and glowed with a special warmth, just as she did. It mattered not that they cost a week's wages, it was a small price to pay for all the love and affection bestowed on one who was not her own. I was sure they would say themselves the things I couldn't put into words.

I had planned to make my presentation the following night, but Death made a sudden call before me and took my very good friend, the Head's wife, away from this life. I found myself, for the first time, holding a tasselled cord and suffering the hurt and pangs of personal loss. How awful it felt to have been too late with my gift.

Thinking about it, until I could stand it no more, I visited the grave that night at the darkening. The air was heavy with the perfume of the flowers on the wreaths as I knelt down and in a hushed voice told of the love I had for her and, easing up a corner of the new laid turf, I gently pressed the beads down through the earth and gave them to her.

As I had promised I wrote home every week and Mother faithfully replied with all the news. But one day I received a letter from my father. Even from the outside it looked important. I didn't have to read between the lines to know that all was well with his world. There was a new Company, registered and launched, with great prospects. He had put my name forward for a Director-ship, and it had been accepted.

His writing trembled with excitement.

"This", he wrote, "is the chance I have always wanted for you".

His spirits were high, I could tell by the upward slope of his writing, but mine plunged to the depths. I knew this was, indeed, an opportunity to better myself, financially and otherwise, that I would probably never have again. It would mean giving up the outdoor life which had become part of me and that I had learned to love.

I told the Head first. He stiffened and assumed his 'on parade' posture but, as I tried to explain, he unbent and understood and, in a voice that told how much he really thought of me, he said,

"This is my year for losing", and turned smartly away so I wouldn't dwell on the glisten in an old soldier's eyes.

I had to report to Her Ladyship, too, who, to my surprise, very gently tried to change my mind. She appreciated, she said, that I would like a home of my own and offered me an attractive house, a beautifully designed Lodge at the west entrance to the estate, all to myself with a housekeeper, chosen by herself as a first class cook to look after me, until, as she put it,

"You meet the girl of your choice".

Sorely tempted, I shook my head quickly, not daring to give myself the chance to reconsider and thanked her just the same.

Her Ladyship had been prepared for this and rang for the butler, who brought in a present which she handed to me. It was a leather wallet, with my initials on it in gold, and surprised me again by saying,

"It will be needed. You are going to make your mark".

So, I left gamekeeping and the way of life I loved, left my friends, left my beat on the shore, left the sea with its haunting sounds and left the seagulls to do the crying.

8

I had barely time to warm my seat in the boardroom when, for me, the best laid schemes were suddenly blown apart by billowing war clouds. They moved in, overloaded with their cargo of tears and heartache. Clouds that carried before them an all-embracing mist of feverish excitement that tested reason to the limit but, mercifully, held an anaesthetic to dull the deep surgery to come. Man's inhumanity to man was about to be demonstrated all over again.

There was no scarcity of jobs now. The money flowed to build tanks and planes and all the devilish accoutrements that went with them. Incessantly, voices that screamed loudly about the enemy which was about to annihilate us all and urged us to defend ourselves, our families and the land of our birth.

It was heady stuff and the young men and the young women marched away and I marched with them and, in doing so, found myself in a strange place in a strange land. There was a long hut with rows of beds and rows of fellows about my age who came down from Devon, Somerset, Birmingham, Newcastle, Norfolk, Suffolk, all speaking English in accents I found difficult to understand.

We had just been issued with our uniforms and I teetered from one leg to the other in my efforts to don the long, blue, trousers. The boys in the billet fell about laughing and I finished throwing the offending garments up to the rafters. I put on the blue tunic and buckled on my kilt and, setting my cap at a jaunty angle, strode out the length of the billet, spun round, saluted and strode back again. The boys' cheers rang in my ears but suddenly switched off to an awesome silence. Framed in the doorway was the fearsome figure of the Sergeant.

"You", he roared, "take off that skirt".

I was affronted and said defiantly, "It's not a skirt. It's my kilt".

The sergeant had a wad of papers in his hand. He selected one and waved it about for all to see.

"This", he said, "is a Charge Sheet, No. 252, and you", pointing at me, "are on a charge".

Tersely, he asked for my name and number then, with vicious stabs of his pen, he added, 'Improperly dressed'.

The boys couldn't have been more sympathetic and led me to a friendly camp tailor who, for a small consideration defied all regulations. He ripped up my drainpipe trousers and sewed, into the inside legs, large fillets of the same blue cloth which tapered from my ankles to the tops of my legs. This resulted in a senior service bell-bottomed effect which, being more comfortable and different compensated me somewhat.

When I slept that night I dreamt this was only a dream, but awoke to stark reality and the nightmare of being hounded from pillar to post. The sergeant was with us again with our final issue which included one pair of airman's drawers.

He held up a pair of long, woolly, underpants that I felt should only be offered to great-great-great grandaddy. I could contain myself no longer and allowed myself the luxury of a deep chuckle. The sergeant outdid the action of a spinning top.

"Who laughed?" he asked in a thunderous voice.

The silence was long and painful and the sadist with the chevrons on his sleeve spoke again.

"If I don't find out this instant I will march you all to the guardroom".

I found time to admire the attitude of my fellow airmen. They all knew I was the offender but not one uttered a word and it brought a lump to my throat to know they were prepared to march to the guardroom on my behalf. The sergeant suddenly seemed to take the form of a gigantic bull frog.

"What", he croaked, "is your name and number?"

"I think you have them already".

I gave my pair of drawers to a lad from Ilfracombe who said he would be glad of an extra pair as he was always feeling cold.

This was another mistake on my part as, in the morning, we were marched to the Medical Hut for F.F.I. (Free from infection). It was an examination to ensure we had not been consorting with the wrong type of woman. I created an unwilling diversion when the Medical Officer discovered I was not wearing regulation drawers.

"What", he asked, "have you done with them?"

"I gave them away". That woke him up sufficiently to put me on another charge.

Next came the time of the long needles. Unsuspecting, we shuffled into line and were caught between two desperadoes, the Medical Officer and his first lieutenant. Simultaneously, they administered a jag in one arm for this and a jag in the other for that.

I awoke in the early hours in a feverish sweat. Everyone was running hither and thither to a high-pitched wailing of banshee. It was an air raid warning. The thunder of the ack-ack guns and the deafening crack of the fireballs that the enemy bombers were throwing down sounded as if all hell had broken loose. But, with my arms swollen like rugby balls, I didn't care any more and, in my state of mind, found the whole situation quite remote and about as exciting as cleaning out the canary's cage.

An S.P. (Special Air Force Police) threw open the billet door. The place was suddenly empty, apart from my perspiring, palsified, self. He studied me for a moment then announced, in a shaking voice,

"If you don't get out of that bed and to the shelter this second, you are on a charge".

I groaned a self-commiserating groan. Oh, not again! I just could not get out of that bed and, for the first time in life, didn't care whether I lived or died. But, came the dawn which brought my biggest surprise. I was still alive–and hungry!

Staggering down to the cookhouse was an effort but, when I got there, even the reconstituted egg looked good. I only had time to taste the first spoonful when two very large S.P.s picked me up unceremoniously and marched me away. It was downright degrading.

"Left, right. Left, right." Through the door. "Prisoner and escort. Shun".

I suddenly realised 'The Prisoner' was me and, most ignominious of all, my hat was snatched off. The officer at the desk in front of me flipped idly through my sheaf of 252s and looked up, the right corner of his mouth twitching.

"You are 1014064, Gideon Scott May?"

"Yes", my escort hissed simultaneously, "Sir", and the officer continued,

"You have been in the Royal Air Force three days, eight hours, ten minutes and", he consulted his watch, "forty-five seconds and you are here before me on four separate charges. Do you intend to create records?"

There was no answer to that one.

"Is there anything you wish to say before I sentence you?"

I cleared my throat and said,

"Are there any more Scotsmen in the R.A.F.?"

My judge leaned back in his chair, pushed his hat to the top of his head and slowly said, with all the feeling in the world,

"Scotsmen in the R.A.F.! They run the bloody thing. Case dismissed".

My escorts who, up to now, had behaved like two sanctimonious cats with a mouse trapped between them, looked sour as I retrieved my hat, saluted smartly and scuttled thankfully away.

When I got back to the billet I was immediately surrounded.

"Come on, now, Haggis. Tell us what happened".

"Well", I said, "I met an officer and a gentleman, with a lot of understanding. Do you know what he said?"

There was a long drawn-out, suspense-laden "No-o-o".

I made the majestic hand signal he had made and adopted his tone of finality, "Case dismissed!"

The whole hut exploded, blankets, 'biscuit' mattresses, kit bags, hats, shoes anything that came to hand, was thrown in the air. Anyone passing in those moments would have thought the war was over and won.

That night, at 'lights out' the boy in the bed next to mine (and he was a boy, fresh from school, a clean-cut type called Ronald, with English I had no difficulty in understanding) was kneeling at his bedside with head lowered and hands pressed together under his chin. He was soon spotted and the ribbald comments came thick and fast, interlaced with piercing whistles and catcalls. But Ronald had found someone important to talk to and

121

took not the slightest notice.

I suddenly felt a deep sense of shame, not so much for the others but for myself. I hadn't found the time to pray recently so I, too, knelt down opposite Ronald and immediately felt better. I could no longer hear the noise and gave thanks for being looked after and expressed the fervent hope that the folks at home were not being forgotten and ended 'for Jesus Christ's sake'.

I looked up. Ronald was the only one to have tucked himself in bed. The rest were all kneeling at their bedsides in a long, penitent, line.

The next morning we were lined up for selection, my 'civvy street' title of company director stood me in good stead, and I was picked to join a privileged few for immediate training. The rest, amid moans and groans were relegated to guard duties and fatigues. I made an instant resolve to work and study hard and win some of those chevrons for my arm, not to give it more power, just to get a bit of peace and quiet for myself.

I got the coveted stripes all right, in triplicate, and the only posting to Northern Ireland.

It was a stormy sea journey but, blessed with a tummy that lifted and fell peaceably with the ocean swell, I watched the soldiers gallantly escort the ladies of the A.T.S. to the heaving side of the boat and join them in their 'kit inspection' overboard. I was joined by a ship's officer.

"Ah", he said, "I see you have the way of it, with one leg to port and the other to starboard. The ship is like a lady who must have her own way—just ride with her". So we stood in the heavy swell and moved in unsion, until the new day grew upon us. "There", he continued, pointing to the horizon, "there she is looking after us".

"Who is 'she'?"

"She is a destroyer, belonging to the Royal Navy," he

answered in reverent tones.

We disembarked on the Emerald Isle and I could see, now, the origin of its name and why it was so given. It was all due to the generous amount of water it received from above.

I reported to the aerodrome and was directed to the Field Kitchen for a meal. I splashed my way through the muddy swamp. A plate was thrust into my hands, a fried egg flipped on to it from one side landing, miraculously, right way up with a rubber bounce, followed by a shower of soggy chips from the other side, and the raindrops danced a fizzing Irish Jig in the hot grease.

In the corner of a sodden tent I ate my meal, sharing it with a starving Irish Wolfhound, and reflected that there wouldn't be much action in this part of the world. I couldn't have been more wrong.

The first squadron had just taken delivery of three flights of planes. "A" flight had a red boss to the propellor, "B" a yellow one and "C", the flight that I was assigned to, had blue.

My first night as Duty Officer I shared with a cheerful Cockney character called Vic, and we had a visit from an enemy marker plane that droned around us ominously. I lifted the phone and alerted all personnel on duty. We had no defences and could only wait to see what was going to happen. I had the feeling that someone else had found out about the arrival of the new planes and our visitor up above revealed all, by dropping a ring of flares around the drome. Soon it was bright enough to read a newspaper outside but we didn't, we retreated to the Armoury!

Suddenly I remembered the guard on the Bomb Dump. I lifted the phone.

"Bomb Dump guard?"

"Yes, yes", a voice quavered. "Any orders?"

"Yes, get to hell out of it".

Vic started to sing. I learned, afterwards that he always sang when really agitated. It was a cockney song,

"Up the apples and pears, through the rory-o-mor, back to me dear old trouble and strife, on the cane and able, you will see a pair of Jack the rippers, and a cup of rosy lea . . . "

I was trying to interpret all this when the door blew in and, wedged in its middle, was a large chunk of smoking, hot, bomb casing. Vic was outraged.

"Jock, what are we going to do?"

It was a warm summer night but I had never felt so cold. Even the bombs, screaming hideously and exploding thunderously, ceased to shake me. I picked up a Lewis gun and, pointing to the mounting said,

"Bring that and the 'ammo' pans".

We set the gun up outside. Vic steadied the mounting whilst I clapped on a drum of cartridges. I had the fleeting thought that there never was a firework show such as this.

A plane shed its bomb load and turned again to come in low with its guns blazing.

"The basket will see us if you fire too soon", hissed Vic. "Wait till he's almost over us".

I waited until it was almost overhead and poured a stream of bullets into the belly of duck-egg blue. It disappeared into the night, leaving behind a trail of curling, black, smoke. We watched and waited. Away to the west there was a last 'woof' and a lurid flash of flame licked upwards to light up the sky. Then for a few moments a strange stillness hung over all, the calm after the storm, to be broken by the wails of the fire engines and ambulances.

"The blood waggons make the most hellish noise", observed Vic.

We lost most of our planes that night, destroyed on their dispersal points. We lost a lot of men, too.

The cleaning-up was a heart-rend ing sickening business. But there was a diversion–the exuberance over the crashed German bomber. The Motor Transport sergeant brought in a large piece of the wreckage and mounted it outside the Armoury door. I knew I had seen it before–it was bullet-ridden, duck-egg blue.

The following night we were trying to catch up lost sleep, when an old Irish farmer burst into the billet. Vic's bed was nearest the door and the old man seized him by the shoulder and shouted in his ear,

"Them ruddy Germans have dropped a bomb in my field and" dropping his voice very low, "I can hear it tickin'."

Vic pushed him away, sleepily but, trying to console, said,

"If it's still ticking it's all right".

The old man gave up at that and disappeared into the night. A muffled voice came from under Vic's blankets.

"My life, that one wouldn't know the difference between a 'ticken' and a 'turkey', and his bed shook with fiendish Cockney laughter.

There was no laughter next morning. The old farmer had been to the Wing Commander, who summoned me before him.

"You're fresh from school and must know all about bombs. Take an N.C.O. and deal with it."

I took Vic. That wiped the smile from his face.

There were delayed bombs about all right. We had just received word that the latest big bang was the new Motor Transport shed that had just blown up. No one had noticed the round hole in its roof. There was another big hole in the middle of Farmer Flacherty's field.

I looked down the hole and saw the bomb was there all

right. I studied my timetable of delays; the latest information was that the enemy's timings were much the same as our own and there was still plenty of time for this one to go off. I looked at Vic.

"Have you prayed lately?"

"No," he said, "but I'm starting right now".

Together we dug down, and around, the bomb. It brought a chill to this beautiful day and I wondered if the skylark's song would be the last sound I would hear. It seemed such a pity to die on a day like this, so I got busy while time was still on my side, placing a slab of explosive in the bomb while Vic ran out a long roll of wire. I fixed my end to the detonator, plugged it into the explosive and scrambled quickly out of the hole.

I checked it carefully. There must be no slip up here. For a second I couldn't see Vic, then I spotted him hugging the green grass. In one motion I pressed down the plunger and threw myself flat. The resulting explosion heaved the earth beneath us, rocked the Irish hillside, showered us with earth and stones and sent the seagulls fluttering wildly in the sky like agitated, elongated, pieces of paper.

Vic, down first, was up first, dancing around like a dervish. Farmer Flacherty was racing towards us, a big stone jar of potheen cradled in his arms.

"Bhoys O bhoys," he gasped, "and weren't you the ones that blew Satan out of me field".

He pulled the cork, we could tell by the sound it was only for 'specials'.In turn we tipped the jar back and drank deeply. It had a sweet, syruppy taste and immediately made life into a mellow, lethargic, place.

"Come into the house now, me bhoys" said Flacherty and, shouting through the doorway, "Bridget, we will now have the bacon, eggs, and potato bread, if you please".

I looked up at the blue sky–it was, indeed, a beautiful day.

The wait for plane replacements was filled in by various activities. All air gunners were ordered to report for extra training methods. Vic told me exactly what would happen. The adjutant, Squadron Leader Wiggal would shoot first, but before that, he would say,

"Just for fun, lads, let's each put half a crown in the kitty", and, so saying, tossed his coin into a dormant, upturned, clay pigeon. Everyone was allowed ten birds. The adjutant finished with a score of nine, blew the smoke out of his gun, and departed.

"The basket" Vic breathed in my ear, "will be back to collect at the finish. He always does".

The kitty was quite considerable. There were thirty six air gunners, the adjutant, Vic and myself and, dutifully, each dropped his half crown into the kitty and 'had a go'. I was drawn last of all and, unlike the other boys had 'done it all before'. Also, unlike the adjutant, I felt I was cheating. I spread the ten 'birds' into dust over the sky.

Vic collected the money and babbled, "It's all yours, Jock".

"All right, boys" I shouted, "the beer is free in the mess tonight as long as the kitty lasts".

Everyone went wild with delight, except Vic, "Wiggal is not going to like this, he's not going to like it at all". He proved to be dead right.

We were assigned to special duty next day. The briefing was short, sharp and to the point. Twelve transports were to proceed to an old Irish castle, a secret rendezvous, to collect the bombs and the ammunition that were stored there. On no account were we to stop. There were those who could be looking for this convoy, so I buckled on my revolver and tried to look as though I had done it all before.

Vic led, and said, "Just follow me, Jock and do as I do". So he went ahead with the first six transports and I followed on behind in the leading cabin of my six. Everything went well until we were on the road back when, suddenly, all the vehicles came to an abrupt stop, like shunting railway trucks. I climbed out of my truck and there was Vic, holding up four big, brawny, military policemen at pistol point.

"Back up, Jock" he shouted so I, too, drew my pistol. "The baskets (this was his favourite expression when excited) tried to stop us".

It was indeed, a military checkpoint, and the Irish civilians in their cars, were laughing their heads off at the sight of the Provost Marshall's top police patrol with their hands in the air. In that moment, I vowed that never again, would I listen to the voice of an excited Cockney. But I 'backed up' and we waved the lorries through and, jumping aboard the last one, gave the M.P.s the R.A.F. salute!

Before we reached the 'drome the communication lines were red hot, and next morning Vic and I marched to the C.O.'s room. I went in first, but the C.O. wasn't there! He was on leave and, sitting smugly in his seat, was the adjutant, Squadron Leader Wiggal, licking his lean, mean lips.

"We were told not to stop", that was my defence.

Wiggal leaned menacingly forward. "You knew very well that those military police were on His Majesty's Service".

I protested further they could have been anyone dressed up.

"Poppycock" sneered Wiggal. I could tell that the clay pigeon episode had burned deeply, specially as his half crown contributed towards the free beer. He was speaking again.

"Consider yourself lucky not to be stripped of your rank. Reprimanded."

The sheer injustice of it all nearly choked me. Vic took a more philosophical line. "Well", he said, "what's getting you? We're free ain't we?"

I asked to see the C.O. when he returned.

"Well", he said, "what's done is done. I am told the Army had to be appeased", and his eyes twinkled. "But it wasn't such a bad show, was it Jock? Besides, it's a good thing to keep your name popping up at Records, especially when they read your charge sheets. It could bring you promotion. When it comes to a tangle with the Army, the R.A.F.'s a very understanding outfit!"

Unknown to both of us, there was another big tangle on the way. The replacement planes were slow to come and schemes and diversions were planned. The mechanics had worked hard and four of our remaining planes were declared serviceable, and were despatched to Lough Neagh for "air to ground" target practice.

This all sounded really Irish to me as the firing would be into the water. On this occasion, I had been delegated as Safety Officer on what turned out to be one of the unsafest exercises I had known. My task was to check two floating targets before and after the planes had fired at them. To do this, I had to accomplish the fantastic acrobatic feat of jumping from the rescue launch to the target and back again, judging the rise and fall of the waves to a split second.

I was marking the last pilot's score and conscientiously counting each bullet hole and I knew the next plane was due to fire at the target half a mile to my left. I gave it a glance–nothing was there. I turned around. The plane was there all right, sweeping low and straight for the target I was clinging to!

It was one of these nightmares that render the

movement of limbs impossible; there is the desperate urge to scurry from terror but the legs refuse to function and, anyway, I had nowhere to run. The terror grows and grows until you scream out loud. I screamed my heart out, but didn't wake up to find it was all a dream. The plane was growing bigger and bigger. With an arm, seemingly loaded with lead, I pulled the Verey pistol from my belt and fired, just as the first stream of bullets danced their way towards me over the water.

The double red explosion of the Verey gun blinded me, temporarily. The plane ceased firing, swooped over me, turned in a steep bank and, coming back, waggled its wings apologetically, and flew away. I signalled for the launch, jumped aboard and went away, too. I had experienced all the target practice I wanted for one day.

But there was another day and more practice. This time it was 'air to air' which involved one plane towing a target, a long, white drogue; another plane having a go at it; and another count of bullet holes when we got down. I still wore the mantle, or carried the burden, of Safety Officer. Vic was singing as he fastened up the gear.

"What's the matter?" I asked him, attuned now to his every mood.

"Some of these blokes couldn't hit a cow in the backside with a shovel", he observed moodily. "And there's something else. For God's sake, look out. Old Wiggal is the first to shoot".

I had the feeling that Wiggal had it in for me, he was the brooding type and had lost face over the clay pigeon shoot. I hoped fervently that he didn't have the powers of concentration of a man I had seen on a film, who could shatter a pane of glass just by looking at it, or, by the power of his mind think buildings into collapsing or cause a plane to fall out of the sky.

The thought of that final effort was with me when I saw Wiggal coming in on his first run and I let the drogue run out another fifty yards, trying to be on the safe side. The bursts from the Browning guns were far too high, seemed almost purposeful and buzzed like swarming bees over my head. I did not appreciate Wiggal's sense of humour and, to remove all further temptation, I tripped the target's release gear and it floated down, leisurely, over the little Irish town.

Back at the 'drome, Wiggal was there before me making nasty jokes about blokes with finger trouble. But our ever-understanding C.O. said,

"Go and pick up the drogue, Jock, and we'll call it a day".

We toured the streets of the town until I spotted it, wrapped lovingly around a set of chimney pots. I knocked gently on the house door, then, again louder. Eventually, and ever so reluctantly, it opened to expose the business end of an Irish blunderbuss, grinning with an expectant gleam. Behind it, squinting along the barrel, I could just discern the features of an elderly lady. I cleared my throat,

"Madam, we are the Royal Air Force".

There was silence for a moment as the blunderbuss was slowly lowered and the old lady, shaking with emotion said,

"The Lord be praised that you have come. There's a German on my roof".

Sweeping my hat off and bowing low I allayed her fear.

"Madam, your troubles are over. We have come to collect him. Just stay inside a little longer and everything will be all right".

I could hear Vic mocking in the security of the transport.

"Hoots, woman. This is the Rroyal Airr Forrce, ye ken", and the vehicle shook with hilarity. I was not amused and sent him on the roof. It was quite a high one.

"That", I thought, "will knock some of the nonsense out of his head".

But, echoing around the chimney pots I could still hear that devilish, cheerful, Cockney laughter.

He was bubbling over with it next morning.

"Jock", he said, I just heard in the Orderly Room that the top Army Brass has been to visit the C.O. His men, apparently, are due to be sent overseas and he would like to lay on some entertainment for them. Perhaps a boxing match. And our C.O. agreed to a match between the Army and the R.A.F."

After the Army Brass had left, the C.O. sent out orders that those competing would be excused duty for three days for training and would be fed on grilled beef steaks.

"We couldn't miss that, could we, Jock? So I've put both our names down.

"You did, what?"

"Now don't panic, Jock. It's too late for that, they're up on the board".

I had never boxed before but Morgan, in the past, had grudgingly praised my right arm. I did not really enjoy the steaks, they became pieces of cottonwool as I thought of things to come.

The Big Night did come and the arena was constructed in the centre of the aerodrome; a small square of ropes and canvas toasting in a battery of lights, surrounded by a sea of bodies, their round faces polished by the moonlight and the intake of pints of Guinness, from barrels donated by a local brewery. They call it Porter because, I thought, it was always ready to carry you off.

I could have done with some, but combatants were not

allowed any. This was a series of eliminating bouts and the packed crowds of soldiers and airmen growled the growls of animals awaiting the kill.

Vic was knocked down to roars of approval from one side and shouts of "Get up" from the other but, sensibly, I thought, he didn't get up and saved himself from becoming a 'demolition' job. But he had the strength to cheer loudly when his opponent was beaten in the next round.

Miraculously, I won two fights in succession, due mainly to my good arm which I stuck out at intervals and my opponents kept running into!

It came round to the final bout. The night was filled with tension, cigarette smoke and the dark, treacly, fumes of Guinness. As I sat in my corner I knew just how the gladiators must have felt. But, at least, if I got beaten I wouldn't have to die.

I had a look in the other corner and wasn't so sure. He was a tall, gangling fellow with a fixed, confident grin. The bell rang and, to the roars of the crowd, I exchanged punches with my opponent in the centre of the ring, each trying to get the measure of the other. He was certainly big, with a guard and a reach that I could not answer, and he pummelled me mercilessly for two rounds.

It was the third and last round. Vic was in my corner rubbing me briskly with a towel and wringing his hands.

"Oh, Jock," he moaned, "you're in a bit of a mess".

I felt battered and blood from a cut above my eye was blinding me. I could taste the overflow, it was sticky and salty.

"Jock", Vic whispered huskily, "there's only one thing to do — rush him and aim for the bread basket".

My lips were swollen, making words difficult, so I nodded. As the bell went I charged across the ring. My opponent tried to push me away but I was under his arms and, with all the remaining strength in my tired body, I sank my fists into the pit of his stomach. With a surprised look he doubled up and crumpled to the floor.

The Referee pointed a large and accusing finger at me and waved me to my corner, seized a microphone and announced in a loud voice,

"The Blue Corner is disqualified".

There was a resounding roar of approval from the Army contingent and an equally loud howl of outrage from the R.A.F. and then the fighting really started. The entire aerodrome was a seething mass of struggling bodies as waves of blue and khaki threw themselves at each other in combat. The Military Police and Special R.A.F. Police went into action, too, but were overwhelmed and many a grudge was sorted out in the process.

The Commander appealed over the address system, but he either wasn't heard or was ignored in the general pandemonium. It took the Fire Brigade and a full half hour of hosing the combatants, together with a sudden state of exhaustion, to restore peace.

Later, when Vic was attending to my various injuries he said, full of consolation,

"Never mind, Jock, cheer up, you didn't lose", and added with his eyes glowing, "What a finish! The Army versus the R.A.F. Did you ever see such a fight?" Throwing back his head, he laughed and laughed. I tried to laugh, too, but it hurt.

The fighting continued over the next two days, but it was legalised, now, under the name of Military Manoeuvres. Information filtered through that the Inniskilling Fusiliers, as an exercise, were going to take over the aerodrome. Our orders were to repel all 'invaders'. A ring of defence was hastily arranged around the perimeter and I was placed in charge of a machine gun nest and, together with the rest of the squadron, waited.

"These characters", observed Vic morosely, "never come from where they are expected".

He was right. Out of a cunning, billowing, smoke screen they charged forward, in a screaming, bayonet pointing, hellish horde, wave upon wave.

"Wait, Jock", urged Vic. "They're trying to frighten us. Just let them come within twenty yards and we'll give them the fright of their lives".

I crouched low behind the machine gun, it was a Browning and could fire much faster than the tick of a second. Vic fed in the long belt of ammunition and I pulled back the breech to engage the first round.

They were now so close I could see the whites of their glistening, glittering eyes and teeth of the blackened grimacing faces.

"Let them have it, Jock!" hissed Vic and, at the touch of my finger, the gun became a live thing. Although the cartridges were blanks theirs was no idle chatter as, at this range, the sting of the powder and scorch of the flame sent the front ranks reeling.

The Umpires had already ruled that we had accounted for over fifty 'dead', but one of the 'dead' paid no attention to being ruled out. He jumped over our parapet, struck me in the chest with his gun, knocking me flat on my back, and stuck his bayonet at my throat.

"Where's the cookhouse?" he roared.

The C.O. was right, my promotion came through, together with a posting to an R.A.F. Station in England. It was my last night in Ireland.

"There's a big dance in Belfast, tonight", Vic told me.

We began at the Ulster Sports Club, where you select your own steak and, while it was cooking, played a game of billiards and had a drink. Vic ordered three whiskies and we drank each other's health.

"Whose is the other one?" I enquired.

"It's for my Dad", croaked Vic. "I had word this morning that I had lost the Old Man".

I thought, how typical of the Cockney to keep his great sorrow bottled up underneath a cheerful grin. I bought another three whiskies and, again, we drank each other's health then, raising the other glass, I said,

"To your Dad", and tipped it back.

After our meal we went to the dance hall. There was no scarcity of young lassies but the men, mostly wearing civilian clothes, did not look very friendly as we danced with their girls. I suppose you couldn't blame them, our being 'foreigners' and, as Vic passed, he whispered,

"Don't push your luck, Jock, just play it cool".

I was, in fact, feeling very warm and slipped outside for a breath of air. A fine drizzle revealed itself in the lamplight and, as I bathed in its coolness, two men sprang out of the night and seized my arms in a vice-like grip. Another was at my back with one arm in a choking grip around my throat, the other arm holding a gun that bored into the centre of my back.

The men bundled me into a car that set off with a roar, its tyres screeching as we made a sudden turn off the main street. I just got a glimpse of the street name. It was Falls Road. The name meant only one thing to me — Forbidden Territory. That was one of the first things I was told. Yet, here I was, 'Out of Bounds', and away from the protecting wings of the R.A.F. What was to become of me?

I was soon to know.

The car suddenly bounced to a stop and I was dragged out. My arms were numb from the constant pressure, my throat ached and the metal barrel of the pistol seemed to have worked its way into my backbone. A brilliant light

137

blinded me and the man at my back thundered,

"Bridget, this is the one, isn't it?"

A voice I will remember forever spoke clearly and quickly, with a rich Irish brogue,

"Sure, he is not the one. He is innocent".

Grudgingly, I was released, the gun leaving behind a painful circle in my back. I could just make out the figure of a girl and could only manage to get out three words,

"Thank you, lady".

Somehow, I managed to find my way out of Falls Road and back to the dance hall. Vic was pacing up and down outside. I had never seen him so upset.

"Where the devil have you been?"

I told him and, when I had finished, all the colour drained from his face.

"My life, Jock, you could been 'done in' or, maybe, they were after a shotgun wedding".

There wasn't a chuckle in his voice and neither of us thought it a laughing matter, so we went to the Star and Garter where, after a couple of drinks, I felt the blood come back to my face.

"Vic", I said "we'll have one more with your Dad".

Back at the billet we were in high spirits and Vic helped me to pack my kit.

"Jock, can I try on your skirt?"

"That has to be packed carefully and it's not a skirt, it's a kilt".

"Okay, okay", Vic tried to appease me. "Can I try it on?"

"Be my guest".

Vic took off his shoes, socks and trousers and I buckled the kilt around him. He picked a chair and, cradling it like the bagpipes, marched up and down, the kilt swinging above his skinny, hairy legs. I knew then that Vic was coming to terms with the loss of his father and exchanging his painful grief for an occasional heartache.

We said good-bye in the early morning. Vic was at his expansive best in order to hide his feelings.

"Jock," he said, "you are the very best Scotsman I have ever met", and, after a pause, he added, "Come to think of it you are the only haggis basher I have ever met".

He gripped my hand. "And you're still the best".

On the boat I looked back at Emerald Isle as it receded and vanished in a vale of mist. It had a magic of its own and I promised myself that, when the opportunity arose, I would return.

9

The R.A.F. Station I reported to was a very important one and I wondered why I had been sent there. But in no time, I thought I knew.

Information had come from men who lived dangerously in enemy territory that invasion could be imminent, and aerodromes would be priority targets for specially trained airborne forces, especially this one which was number one on the list. I duly received orders to prepare for demolition anything of importance, from the most advanced aerial equipment to fuel supplies.

As the invasion fever mounted we worked like beavers to foil any 'take over bid' and, very soon, under everything of any value or importance to the enemy, their lay, snugly cradled, a five hundred pound bomb. They were all cunningly wired to one focal point that was to be my battle station overlooking the entire aerodrome and its surrounding buildings.

My second-in-command followed my every movement. He was trained to do my job and shadowed me everywhere, in case, as the orders coldly spelt it out, I fell. Every day we checked the slumbering bombs, the detonators, the wiring and the deadly dynamite exploder. It's plunger waited poised, to take one determined press down to blow the whole place up.

But the expected clouds of mushrooming parachutists never appeared in the sky. The enemy never came, but another posting came for me.

My new squadron was ready for action. When I reported for duty I knew instinctively that, here, there would be no mock battles, everything would be 'for real'. The aerodrome was built on the surface of a dried out lake, there was sand everywhere. It stung your eyes and left a gritty, grinding message in the teeth; lively lizards darted here and there, seeking the shelter of coarse, spiky, tussocks of grass that seemed to fight a losing battle to keep the shifting sand in one place.

The duty sergeant directed me to my billet, its approach had a sandbank decorated with a row of grinning, human skulls.

"Who are they?" I asked, in a voice that I didn't recognise as my own.

"Oh", explained the sergeant, aimiably, "the building contractors dug them up and set them there and, well, you know what superstition is in the R.A.F. Nobody, but nobody, wants to disturb them".

I looked at the dispersal points where the big, black, bomber planes waited, with wings outstretched, like queen bees awaiting the attention of 'the workers'. They were there, armourers, stripped to the waist, stuffing trolley loads of high explosive fodder into the bellies of the bombers. No wonder the skulls were grinning — the whole place smelt of Death.

In the days that followed we were joined by a division of the American Air Force. They brought with them something in the way of light relief and a totally different way of life. They broke every rule in the R.A.F. Book, by wandering into the Mess with their hats off! They slouched around indolently in their flying suits, doing their best to display the motifs on their backs. These ranged from a Red Indian Chief's headdress to some that simply said 'Flack Bait'.

I felt sorry for them. They were putting on a show, but didn't yet know what flack was all about.

But, worst of all, were their eating habits. There was nothing that put me off an honest-to-goodness breakfast of bacon and eggs, than a fellow sitting next to me working his soggy way down a mound of pancakes smothered in hot syrup. There's nothing like being put off your breakfast to put the rest of the day on an upside down plate.

I was still upset when an American pilot engaged me in conversation. Not listening particularly carefully, I came to when he said.

"We are doing the daylights and you are doing the nights". He leaned closer, until I could smell the bourbon on his breath. "It takes guts," he said heavily, "to attack in broad daylight".

I was still suffering pangs from breakfast time and the bacon and eggs and the pancakes were in greasy conflict inside. I felt really mean and said,

"Cissy stuff".

The American was not amused and became affable, like a bear that wants to get closer to give that final all-embracing hug.

"You", he said, "have the Scotsman's kilt". I was amazed the way talk got around. "My month's wages", he continued, "against your kilt, that you don't fly in the nose of my Boston, tomorrow morning".

I gave him a look that suggested I was dealing with a spoilt child and said,

"I'll be there".

It was a bad decision on my part. From the moment of the screaming 'take off' I was subjected to some of the most terrifying moments of my life. As we sped across the Channel I peered down at the water through the perspex dome and the churning waves did their best to rise up and slap me on the face.

As we flew across France the early morning farm workers threw themselves to the ground. I could count the nails on the soles of their boots and their cattle ran

wildly, tails high in the air. The plane rocked, almost lazily, to the left and lifted a wing just in time to allow a farm house to pass underneath.

Worse was to come. We sailed insolently over the muzzle of the big, ack-ack guns and had just a second to look at the white, upturned, faces of their crews.

It was a devil's gallop on wings. We swooped like a hawk on our target but they were ready for low-flying birds and the bullets buzzed around us like bees that have had their nest disturbed.

As the bomb load was released the plane lifted in a moment of sheer relief at shedding its burden. Just then, a bullet smacked through the perspex nose, ricocheted off an aluminium stay and whined past my ear, but it left a stabbing pain in my right eye that burned into my head all the way back. We bounced three times on the runway and I thought the pilot much better at low flying than landing, and he had the audacity to say,

"Well, Scottie, still with us?"

I shook my head from side to side to hide my agony and through clenched teeth said,

"Kindergarten stuff", and made my way hurriedly to the Sick Bay. My eye was driving me to the point of insanity. The flight sergeant at the door greeted me abruptly,

"It's past sick parade".

I brushed him aside, I was in terrible pain and almost threw myself into the arms of the Medical Officer who, fortunately was a man who put suffering as a priority, regardless of uniform, rank or title.

"Where does it hurt?"

I pointed in desperation to my right eye. He produced a bottle and brush and painted my eye and its surrounds, which froze everything in that area to an insensible numbness. With my left eye I watched as he seemed to deposit my right eye ball on to my cheekbone. Then, with a pair of fine tweezers, he drew out a needle-like object, with a deep sigh of satisfaction.

"It's a sliver of lead," he said. "Could have been sheared off the nose of a bullet. But you", he raised his eyebrows, "haven't been under fire today".

I looked blank, particularly with my right eye. He was a very understanding M.O., a fatherly type who you don't forget.

"Right", he said, "I understand". He went on,

"You won't be doing anything for the next forty-eight hours. That's the time it will take for your eye to become unfrozen and back to something like normal".

My relief was unbounded; a release from excruciating pain and the horrifying thought that a report of my escapade might have been placed before our Commanding Officer, Group Captain Wolsencroft. To incur his displeasure was to be damned forever. He was regarded by all ranks as a holy terror, was Groupie Wolsencroft. I sensibly decided he was one to steer clear of, but Fate decided otherwise.

The E.N.S.A. Forces Entertainment Party, due to appear at the weekend, had got lost somewhere between aerodromes. There was a big flap on to raise some alternative entertainment for the troops. Anyone who could do anything had to volunteer, or be conscripted.

The Entertainments Officer had been told that I had a kilt in my kit, and promptly put me on the bill as the Singing Tartan Parachutist. We had a short rehearsal, then he gave me an additional billing for the Grand Finale, as Madame Fifi with Les Girls.

It was the Big Night and the house was packed to suffocation. I was on first with my kilt and a crooked apple tree stick. Wishing something would strike me dead, I sang 'The Wig, wig, wiggle, wiggle, waggle o' the

Kilt' and danced around the stage like a dervish. This got
things off to a cheery, hand clapping start, with its fair
share of catcalls and rude remarks.

This was an all star, all ranks, show, with singers,
conjurors, pianists (the R.A.F. never seemed to lack
pianists) and a magician. But last on the programme was
Madame Fifi and Les Girls — Straight from Paris. The
'girls' were Dusty Miller, Ginger Pegg, Smudger Smith,
Chalky White, Nobby Clark, Taffy Thomas and Buck
Rogers, wearing multi coloured wigs, frilly dresses,
flashing silk stockings, topped off with frothy, frilly,
panties, all donated by the ladies of the W.A.A.F.

As Les Girls danced onto the stage the audience went
wild. The noise was deafening as they roared their
delight, interspersed with piercing wolf whistles, as Les
Girls went through a daring 'Can Can' routine. I was
shocked to realise what fantastic girls they all made! with
the possible exception of Buck whose black hairy chest
sprouted out above his bra as if in protest of his having to
make the ultimate sacrifice and shave off his
magnificent, handle bar, moustache.

Standing in the wings, I took a glance at the stage
entrance mirror. The W.A.A.F.s had really gone to
town and powdered, painted and lipsticked me. I wore a
blonde wig with dangling curls, an off-the-shoulder
shimmering dress with a bra underneath, each cup
holding a large grapefruit. I could feel their suggy kiss on
my breast. To complete the outfit I wore a pair of high
heeled shoes, black mesh stockings and matching lace
knickers.

The Chorus finished their high kicking act with the
splits that, literally, nearly took them apart. As I waited
I reflected on the briefing I had received from every long
suffering officer in the Squadron. There were so many of
them but there was only one selected as 'the target for

tonight', Group Captain Wolsencroft.

It was take-off time and as Les Girls danced off stage I took a deep breath which my grapefruits resented. Clutching the microphone I tripped daintily on to the stage. The whistling was deafening and completely drowned the beginning of my song, but I carried on regardless.

"Some of these days
You're gonna miss me, honey,
They were listening now.
"Some of these days
You're gonna be so blue,
My timing had to be perfect.
"You're gonna miss my huggin',
You're gonna miss my kissin',

I was making my way down off the stage and could hear the hiss of hundreds in indrawn breaths that tried to guess where I was going.

"You're gonna miss me, honey,
When I'm far away,

I knew exactly where I was going and playfully pinched the cheek of the Wing Commander as I passed him.

"You'll feel so lonely,   For me dear, only,

I was right on target and plumped on to Groupie's lap, my arms around his neck and, breathing heavily into the microphone,

"Oh, you're gonna miss me,
Dear Old Woollensocks".

The orchestra went through the National Anthem three times before a semblance of order was restored. By this time I had made my escape backstage where there was a riot of hilarity.

"Oh ho ho", chuckled the Adjutant, "Old Groupie doesn't know whether he is punched, bored or counter sunk".

In deep, the Group Captain's hard exterior seemed to have been demolished on being acquainted of his nickname publicly, and, in the days to come, it seemed to bring a mellowness that made him a great deal easier to live with.

The next evening, I was detailed for all night duty. For me, this was one of the worst jobs of all, picking the bones of a meal you had no part in, and could sometimes develop into the uneasy business of just waiting.

It was four o'clock in the morning and all the planes were back except S for Sugar, a plane with the reputation 'too sweet to survive', but we had a garbled message that Sugar was shot up but limping home, hopefully in time for breakfast.

The Signals Officer brought me a cup of cocoa. I had met her before. We never spoke but managed to carry on conversations without saying anything. She was a girl who retained her femininity in uniform, I watched her walk away through the steam of the cocoa mug, then cradled my head in my arms and resigned myself to the waiting.

I dreamt I was in the arms of the Signals Officer; her distinctive perfume was in my nostrils and her long, blonde, hair fell over and around me. I was in her arms all right and she was shaking me violently,

"Jock, Jock, wake up. Sugar is coming in on fire!"

At once I was fully awake and quickly alerted the Fire and Ambulance Stations and raced out onto the runway. Sugar was coming in from the east like a fiery comet and touched down with two engines and part of the port wing ablaze. It was like a bonfire night with the gun turret ammunition exploding in all directions and the tracer and incendiary bullets darted into the night buzzing like giant fireflies.

THE KILT FOR KEEPS

Flight Lieutenant 'Timmy' really distinguished himself, having a way of tackling flamers. He was a dab hand at burning planes, was Timoshenko. He always collected the most fearsome burns but, on this occasion, we all had our fair share and were consigned to hospital. I was detained 'indefinitely, with burns, shingles and shock', in that order.

There was visiting in the evening and the boys from my flight came to see me. After paying their respects and eating the fruit at my bedside, they settled down to a card game on my bed but melted away at the approach of the Signals Officer.

"I've been posted", she said. "I had to see you before I left".

The bandages around my eyes were suddenly very moist as she searched my face with her lips for a space, and kissed me.

"I won't forget you", she said, and turned away.

I never forgot her.

The hospital was a world of its own. A clean, polished, antiseptic haven, a shelter from cares, responsibility and the blood of battle, where days passed unnoticed and the nights were long, when exhaustion finally served up its nightcap of sleep, turning it into a nightmare.

Frank, a navigator from British Guiana, was in the next bed. He was dark and husky but quickly turned to a pale grey when I launched into an attack of the 'horrors'. I had a recurring dream that I was trapped in a cone of fire that roared towards me in great flaming scarlet and orange circles, scorching me with a thousand tongues.

"Wake up, Jock. Wake up, for God's sake, wake up."

Frank, shaking and pummelling me banished the nightmare but replaced it with sleeplessness. Also suffering the results of my horrendous dreams, lying on the other side of my bed, was an airgunner, by the name

149

of Marconi. He had a black silk dressing gown with a red dragon; he also had an electric shaver and a father with a chain of ice cream shops. He, like Frank, was heavily burdened with my nightmares and so, after Lights Out, I did my best to make amends by recounting the days that really mattered to me when I was patrolling the coast of the Solway.

I told them how I had made friends with the porpoises, described all the different birds that flocked to feed on the harvest left by the outgoing tide, of hearing the haunting whistle of the otter calling to his mate, and describing the capers of their kits. I told them of the big, brown, female adder which swallowed her young, temporarily, when danger threatened and the woodcock which tucked its chick between its leg and flew to safety.

Frank and Marco listened because, I suppose, it was better than being frightened to death if I fell asleep! Until, one night, after a long pause, it suddenly seemed all worth while when a voice, from the other end of the ward, said,

Jock, tell us again about the wild geese flying across the moon".

In my hospital bed I learned about my father's sudden death and of my mother who, broken-hearted, had followed him. Grief is a heartache that you learn to live with so, for me, there was to be no 'coming home' but, in the stillness of the night, I dedicated myself to rebuilding the Home, and I would do it on the land and in the open air that I loved.

10

Our Medical Officer had a good look at me and decided I was now fit for sick leave and sent me home, but 'home' wasn't there any more and, for the first time, I felt the chill of loneliness.

Just by chance, I met Irralee on Princes Street. She was on leave, too, from the Land Army.

"Why the Land Army?" I asked.

"Well," she said, "my father wanted me to join the Wrens, leading to a commission but there was no place on board ship or off for my pony. And, talking about ponies", she continued, "there's a super horse film on at The Regal tonight".

So I took her and we joined a long, long, queue. In my early R.A.F. days, I had vowed to myself, as I shuffled slowly in line with a knife, fork and spoon clutched in my hand, that I would never ever join a queue again. But I did it this time, for Irralee, so that she could see Old Smokey. During the film she never uttered a word but sat, wide-eyed, as hordes of wild horses poured across the screen, with flying manes and tails in a never ending stream.

We had supper in the Cafe afterwards. Irralee didn't say much–she was still 'away on the range' and ordered bacon and beans! I took the chance to tell her of my plans for the future, to claim a living from the land. I also asked, tenderly, if she would consider sharing such a life with me.

If Irralee was shaken by the suggestion it didn't affect her appetite! Between mouthfuls, she admitted that the idea had its attractions but confided that she would be hard put to it to stand the sight of me all day. As she was thoughtfully putting the last forkful of bacon and beans into her mouth I played my trump card.

"There would be", I said, "a paddock for the pony".

Irralee raised her eyes and looked directly into mine. She was interested!

We had a quiet wedding, except for a choir of sparrows which congregated round the window of the Manse and chirruped loudly as we took our vows. I returned to my squadron, feeling that I had, indeed, taken the first positive step towards making a home.

One day the prevailing wind that had been looked for so long blew the war clouds away and left everyone blinking in the peaceful sunshine, not knowing whether to laugh or cry. The crying I knew was a pain that racked me inside, but I had finished with that and knew where I was going. I said a final good-bye to my R.A.F. blues, buckled on my kilt and faced the world with only my gratuity in my sporran.

My directorship was in abeyance as the company had been closed and showed no signs of reopening, so I picked up the threads of the business my father had left behind and wove them to a conclusion. It entailed a period of waiting for my dream of freedom, but I never grew tired of waiting. Fortunately, Irralee didn't either.

From the beginning of our marriage she had declared her intention of having her children as soon as possible and, as Irralee always means what she says, went into production right away.

Shortly after the arrival of our third little one she came running towards me, wildly waving a copy of *The Courier* and, in a rational moment I managed to decipher her back-to-front, excited, machine-gun talk. The Duke of Atholl's Estate was offering for sale a fifty acre farm on the banks of Loch Tummel. It was the home we had waited for and, miraculously, it had waited for us!

We had a warm, Highland, welcome. A neighbour from Tomintianda had swept the floors, polished the old fashioned grate, complete with 'swee' and had a glowing fire burning. On the hearth was a pile of logs and, so thoughtful, a pile of kindling for the morning. From Lick, straight across the water, came lovely brown eggs which would help 'until we got settled' and indeed they did. And more was to come! We felt at home already.

Later that evening there was a knock at the door. It was the deerstalker and his wife from Duntanlich, apologising because they were late with gifts–turnips, potatoes and a pint of goat's milk. They had rowed over from the other side of the loch in the black dark of a moonless night. Their coming was a valued moment. They didn't stay long, but paused to wish us well and the stalker's wife turned before she disappeared into the night and said,

"You will be the lucky ones. The sun will shine on Croft Douglas when we, on the other side, will be in darkness".

She was right. In the winter months the sun rose only high enough to warm the land on the north side of the loch, gently touching humans and animals alike, making them move appreciatively under their skins, leaving the south side watching jealously as it shivered under its icy cold, frost-spangled, blanket.

From our front door we could look up Loch Tummel to the 'fairy hill', Schiehallion, beyond which lay Loch Rannoch and the Moor of Rannoch, away to the peaks in the west. We could also look down at our biggest field. It ran straight down to the water, it was ploughed and ready for liming.

I sought the help of a local contractor. It was the time of year, he explained that everyone had to do everything for themselves, but he would lend me a tractor. His last instructions were,

"Don't let her stop. She's a dour starter!"

It was destined to be the hardest working day of my life and developed into a daylight nightmare as, one by one, I tipped the hundreds of hundredweight bags into the long, wooden, lime barrow and chugged away on yet another bone shaking ride to spread the barrow's contents over the long rows of ploughed land.

I got to know this tractor. It was old-fashioned, deeply scarred with rust, had ideas all of its own and a pipe that puffed out clouds of pungent smoke. It hiccupped, burped and belched at regular intervals and left me choking in its poisonous paraffinny breath. After the tractor had consumed its fifth five-gallon drum, it began behaving downright dangerously, careering up and down the deep furrows, pausing occasionally to rear up, plunge down with an earth shattering bump, then teeter to one side on two wheels, tipsily waving the other two in the air. Only a series of last minute miracles saved a deadly somersault and saw me back to the farmyard to fill the barrow yet again, each bag getting heavier than the last.

Irralee helped me when she could. While two of the little ones clutched their teddy bears and watched wide-eyed, the wee one was laid in a nest of straw between two bales, and I was given a much needed hand with the mountain of bags. Then Irralee brought me bacon rolls and mugs of tea.

I ate the rolls between tipping bags into the hungry maw of the barrow. It was the first time I had tasted bacon liberally spread with lime, which floated everywhere. I was past caring and washed it down with the tea. I couldn't close my eyes in case they stuck together and I daren't sit down for fear of collapsing so I took yet another perilous ride on the fiery paraffin-pickled monster.

Each time I was certain I had reached the limit of human endurance I gritted my teeth, which wasn't difficult as they were coated with lime. I stumbled wearily on, my legs buckling under me with the weight of the bags and I took out the last of them in a darkness lit only by the red mist before my eyes.

Somehow I got back to the house and collapsed into the big chair. Irralee sponged my face repeatedly but I failed to surface for my supper and slept well into the next morning. When it was ready we harvested the field of golden corn and, though I forgot the number of stacks that were built from that bumper crop, I shall never forget the number of lime bags, and the body racking effort that went into that one day, to nourish the land.

We were newcomers to the Highlands and the way of life, new to the business of making a living from the land, but we were quick to learn. We had to be with our limited resources. We daringly experimented, too, and were the first in the Strath to 'out winter' cattle. The eyes of the farmers and the crofters were upon us and the winter promised to be no light-hearted affair.

With its very first breath it blew one of the worst snow storms we had ever experienced. I had waited most of the day, hoping that the howling winds would eventually tire, but the late afternoon only saw an increase in their fury.

So I set off in the swirling, blinding, snow to check my hairy friends. The stinging snowflakes fell endlessly from the sky and were augmented a thousandfold by the dust of those which had already fallen on the hilltops, only to be gathered up again by the wind, wildly wielding a million broomsticks, and swept viciously down to fill the sheltered valleys.

Gasping, I reached the woods and paused for breath. Away on the windward side I heard the last dying groan of a tree which had reached its limit of endurance and fallen, crashing befoie the storm. But here, in this shelter, were the cattle, grouped silently together, calmly waiting until the elements had had their way.

I counted them. One missing! I counted again. It was Eurach Dearg (Red Lady). I made a large circle, certain she couldn't be far away. Round and round, deeper into the thickets, I went. Where could she be? Time was ticking away and the light going from the sky. In the woods, where the snow threw off the cloak of darkness, every big stone, every broken stump took on the shape of my lost cow.

Blundering into a deep drift, the snow gripped my bare knees in a clammy clasp that threatened to drain the last vestige of warmth from my body and, as I struggled free, I thought I heard a faint 'Moo'. With icy fingers I gouged the snow from my eyes and there, in front of me, was the "Lady". A white mantle had temporarily robbed her of the title "Red", but I knew her and she knew me so I was amazed to receive a warning toss of the head, clearly indicating,

"That's near enough."

And, lying in front of her, wet and shivering, was our first Highland calf. I was thrilled and appalled in turn. Would it live, pitched out from the snug warmth of its mother onto a bed of freezing snow? But the Red Lady's tongue was working overtime and the little one, with a sneeze and shake of the head staggered to its feet, trembling on spread-eagled legs. The big, rough tongue whipped up the circulation in a nonstop effort and with tottering steps the little, questioning calf searched the

157

hairy flank. There, like a set of bagpipes, standing at attention, was the swollen udder. One of the teats, fat, shining and filled to overflowing, sprayed invitingly and a tremor of excitement ran through the tiny form as it fastened on.

As I watched, life and strength flowed into the calf and, before my eyes, it filled out and bloomed like a flower. In Gaelic whisky is called the water of life. I am now convinced that the Highland cow carries in her bag the very cream of existence. So we called him Stoirm (Storm) and, with the snow for a blanket, he grew and thrived.

Spring came, chickens hatched and I thought it was time Stoirm had his first lesson. When I first put a rope on him he did everything; reared, bucked, stood on his head and, finally, lay down, and when he got up again he was ready, with a little coaxing, to walk by my side. He soon accepted the halter,. and to be led, as part and parcel of growing up to be a bull.

The day he found his voice was another great occasion. It wasn't much of a vocal effort at first, but the roar of a young Highland bull hadn't been heard in Strathtummel for many, many years and there were those who strained their ears to hear him. They didn't have to strain for long. Stoirm's lungs grew with him and soon his bellow reached the length and breadth of the valley and far beyond, and even the big, royal stags, throwing their own fearsome challenges, had to stop and listen to him.

I was leading Stoirm one day (his left horn now spanned my chest) when Bobby, one of our neighbouring farmer friends, remarked,

"It's time you had a humbug on his nose, or one of these days he'll 'do' you. Besides," he continued, "you won't be allowed to show him without one." I hadn't really thought about this, hadn't noticed how big Stoirm had grown. He was no longer a teddy-bear youngster, but on the threshold of maturing into a full-grown bull. So a humbug it had to be. This is used to lead Highland bulls, which are not normally rung in the nose, and is a spring-loaded pincer device which clips into the bull's nostrils and, with a rope attached, ensures full control when handling. We bought one in Perth and I thought it a Chamber of Horrors contrivance. What would Stoirm think of me when I clamped this on his nose? It was new and the spring was strong, would it hurt him too much? I would try it myself first.

Irralee found me just as I mustered up enough courage to clip the monstrosity in my own nose. I felt like a cross between a refugee from a chain gang and a martyred Zulu. The tears trickled down my cheeks, and not from emotion. Irralee laughed herself silly and I took off the humbug, tossed it into a drawer and tried to forget about it.

In the days that followed Stoirm lorded it over all the others. Full of himself, he got more reluctant to be driven into the small paddock for his leading lesson, and when I went to get him he would craftily withdraw to some open space, well away from the sanctuary of trees, fence or dyke, and wait for me. He would then start to growl as if he had been taking lessons from a Bengal tiger, it didn't come from this mouth, but ground around in his brisket in an endless recording. If he thought this wasn't sufficient to scare me, his forefeet would start to plough the land, first one side then the other. The divots and stones flew high in the air, and through the clouds of soil, he would watch to see if my steps were faltering. Not yet, so he produced his trump card, to bury his head in the nearest molehill and, with horrible growls, bob up, his eyes blazing pinpoints in a matting of mud and hair. Growling like thunder he said, quite clearly,

"Now, have you ever seen anything as bloody terrifying as me?"

And to emphasise the point he blew clouds of steam from his nostrils, and I always marvelled that he never managed any means of ignition here, to make a real show. A strong nerve, a lusty swear and a not too unkindly whack with my stick across his bottom and he knew he was beaten.

One day Stoirm, seeing me coming, moved off to the centre of a very steep field, and there took up his position. This was all done so calmly and purposefully, no growling, dressing up or bluffing display of fireworks. I could feel that he had thought up something new. He had!

I was approaching uphill, about ten yards away, when he charged. Certainly, it was a playful, bouncing charge. But who wants to play with many hundredweights of beef, bone and muscle, or end up spitted on those gigantic horns? And they did look formidable as they bore down on me. No matador ever timed a neater last-minute side-step, and the bull smell was heavy in my nostrils.

Realising that he had missed, Stoirm clamped on all his brakes and endeavoured to execute a smart 'about turn', but his momentum was such that he skidded wildly and fell flat, sending a wave of tremors along the ground. This was my moment. Before he had the chance to rise, I waded in with my stick and whacked him mercilessly. He took his licking with pained disbelief and, deciding he had had more than enough, struggled to his feet and fled, trumpeting, to the woods.

The next attempt was a more serious affair. I had finished fixing up a little henhouse to give some of the hens a good range on the hill, and was about to make my way back to the croft when I came face to face with Stoirm. There was nothing unusual in this. I saw him every day, but at this particular moment he was eyeing me with a mixture of astonishment and disbelief. I had no stick! I could see, too, that he had not forgotten that day when I had humbled him, and in front of all the cows, too. That burned deeply in his eyes. He gave me that creamy, self-satisfied, deceptively relaxed look, that a cat wears when it has surprised a mouse just that bit too far from its hole.

I stood my ground, wearing a formidable expression and dared him to do anything other than go about his business, but it didn't work. Slowly, determinedly, he advanced until I was breathing his steaming, triumphant exhalations. I took one step back, and it wasn't for fresh air. Stoirm took one step forward, I took another step back and so it went on like some grotesque one-way dance. I couldn't risk a look round, but all the time my hands were waving madly behind me. The henhouse must be somewhere near now and, propping the door open, was a birch pole.

It is said that if you see the hair on the mane of a Highland bull standing on end, you should be up a tree or in the next parish! One more step, my hand closed lovingly round the pole and in one quick movement, I swung round and struck. The soft birch shattered on Stoirm's crown and disintegrated in a thousand pieces. In this moment I knew that our future relationship had been decided once and for all; knew by Stoirm's stunned expression when he raised his lowered head, that he was thoroughly convinced that I had struck him with my hand. So I shook my fist under his nose and he turned meekly allowing himself to be driven to the catching pens, where I haltered and led him.

I wasn't finished with him yet. Into the croft, a quick

161

rummage in the drawer, back to the pens and I had the new humbug on Stoirm's nose before he knew what had happened. And while the mood was on me, I took him for a long steady walk, at the finish of which, we understood each other completely.

We were the first in Strathtummel to enter a pedigree Highland bull for the Show and Sale at Oban. The neighbouring farmers and crofters called to see and appraise him, and brought with them the warm feeling of belonging. And when they had all decided that he was indeed the one to represent them and the Valley, we realised that our bull no longer belonged to us. He was now 'Stoirm of Strathtummel'.

The day Stoirm said farewell to Croft Douglas dawned with a struggle one cold dark February morning. As I led him up the ramp of the cattle float I felt his shiver of excited bewilderment. Inside he was just a youngster undergoing a strange experience, going out into the world and not knowing why or where. I tied him safely and put some straw around his feet for comfort, hay at his nose, and hoped that any fresh snowfalls would hold off until we had got through the hills, at least. With the hum of hydraulics the ramp went up. The big wheels crunched through the snow, eating up the long miles to Oban, and in three hours we were playing our part with the rest at the pedigree Highland bull sales.

All was hustle bustle and excitement at the showyard and we were ushered by a white-coated attendant to our pen. It bore a large lettered card for all to see, Croft Douglas. Around us were other bulls, the cream of the Highland breed, undergoing a fastidious toilet. So, I too, got busy with brush and comb on Stoirm, making sure he looked as good as the others.

Soon we were called to the show-ring and we both tried very hard not to look like novices. The hair of

Stoirm's forelock fell over his eyes in silken waves, his massive horns were burnished and his red and gold coat flowed down to the magnificent tassel at the tip of his tail. Round and round we went in an endless chain and in the centre stood two judges and stewards.

I had my best foot forward and my best sporran on.

We didn't join the selected few, but I still thought Stoirm was as good as any of them so, back in his pen, I gave him an extra big feed, plaited his tail, bedded him down for the night and wondered what tomorrow and the sale ring would bring.

At this moment a diversion was created by two bulls in adjoining pens who, after a period of growling juicy insults, found that the length of rope on their respective tethering points allowed them to reach each other. Contact sparked off a violent explosion and a first-class battle was soon in progress. The roaring and clashing of horns was heard throughout the building and herdsmen dashed to separate the combatants. Colourful Gaelic oaths were punctuated by whacking sticks to step up the bedlam. Just then, a lady (the owner of one of the bulls) swept regally up to the scene and in cool inquiring tones, which rang clearly through the din, said,

"Is he misbehaving?"

Everyone was aghast. Sticks hung suspended in mid-air, angry shouts were strangled at birth; even the bulls, shattered by this assessment of the situation, ceased their battling and meekly allowed themselves to be retied at a respectable and unreachable distance from each other. Thus descended peace once more and soon, with a series of grunts, the bulls began to lie down.

Stoirm who, like myself, was watching points in a new experience took his cue and went down, too. I tickled his ear, told him I wouldn't be far away and said, "Goodnight."

It was only a short distance to the hotel where I had booked to spend the night and I entered, a stranger in a strange land. How artificial everything seemed. I looked into the dining room—glitter and unreality tied up in a table napkin. I hoped Stoirm didn't feel as lonely as I did.

I walked past a wickedly winking sign, Cocktail Bar. Behind it, the bottles sparkled colourfully, glasses gleamed in impeccable formation, there were no gaps in the ranks of the pickled onions or olives and the barmaid looked out of work. I cleared my throat.

"Nobody thirsty?"

The young lady laughed softly, "They're all at the ceilidh. It's in the ballroom".

Of course. I remembered now, the society was holding its herdsmen's supper tonight. I needed no directions, a piper was blowing his heart out.

I opened the door and the blast hit my eardrums. My entrance was unobtrusive and unnoticed, almost. A big moon face beamed at me.

"Ach, you'll be choining me."

I felt as if I had left the chill of the night and drawn my chair up to a warm fire. Piloted by a huge hand, a bottle pointed unquestioningly at my glass and the amber liquid chuckled all the way to the top.

"Slainte!"

We grinned at each other through the bottom of our glasses. The bottle was pointed my way again. I protested, but to no avail, and surrendered. Relaxing, the plaid of tension and tiredness slipped from my shoulders. The last notes of the pipes clawed wildly around looking for escape, the glasses clinked and clunked like a row of trucks on a shunting train and the tide of conversations rose to flood level.

The Full Moon disposed of three sausage rolls in as

many minutes, then inspected a plate of sandwiches. Those, for the titles at the long, top table, he assured me, were more thickly spread.

From the centre of the long table a figure rose and pounded the woodwork unmercifully, combating the noise till it became a murmur, then complete silence.

"Jamie will now give us a song of the islands."

Jamie, his eyes rolling round the ceiling, poured out the Gaelic, his hefty brogues gently tapping out the rhythm on the parquet floor and at every convulsive heave of his chest the buttons threatened to spray like machine gun bullets. The Full Moon was entranced, the spell of the Gaelic holding him fast. Jamie bowed his head and the applause rolled over him like a thousand drum beats.

The accordion band took over and, as they squeezed out the melody one tapped with the toe, one with the heel and one with both feet. It had the desired effect. Three hundred brogues belted the floor in unison.

When The Selection was over and everyone at the point of exhaustion with the foot stamping a heavy, hairy herdsman rose to sing 'The Dark Island'. I marvelled at the soft, delicate, delivery from such a powerful frame.

"How", I whispered, "does he know when to sing?"

"Wheesht, man", hissed the Full Moon, "he has the Quaich in front of him".

It must be some sort of Highland ritual, I mused. It was, and presently the Quaich, brimming full of whisky, was placed in front of me.

"It chist means", the Full Moon explained in the middle of the fiddler's rendering of 'The Hen's March' "that you are on next. So drink up".

At the last draw of the bow, I rose and, swinging the pleats of my tartan from side to side, sang 'The Waggle o' the Kilt'. The accordions and fiddles silently sought

the key then crept in behind just in time to lend full
blooded support for,
> "I'll never forget the day,
> I went on Royal review.
> The Queen came down to see us
> And Prince Philip was there, too.
> As I marched past the Royal Coach
> Prince Philip shook his head,
> The Queen put on her Royal specs
> And looked at me, and said,
> He's a braw, braw, Hielan' Lad . . . . . . "

Everyone joined in the chorus and the building
rocked. I sat down to find the Quaich refilled and the
Full Moon beaming upon me.

"Man you were chist great. The Quaich is filled again,
that means they are wanting more".

I couldn't believe it.

The Chairman was a man renowned in the cattle
business called Big Ben, and not for nothing. His
gigantic thump on the table sent a tremor through the
multitude, gaining a respectful silence that was almost
frightening.

In the hush that followed I found myself telling the
story of a Highland lad who had watched his parents
grow old before their time, striving to claw a meagre
living from the stony hearted land of their croft. So he set
off to work his passage to America and join the great
rush for gold, his only discoveries being trials,
tribulations and headaches. I warmed to the chorus,
> "There's gold in the mountains,
> Gold in the valleys,
> Gold in the rivers
> And gold in the sea.
> Fortunes are waiting

For men to find them,
But only the heartaches
Are waiting for me".

I finished with a yodel that belonged to me alone, which rose to echo the dangling, tinkling crystals of the great chandelier overhead. The last 'good-nights' were said in the early hours of the morning. How many friends, I wondered, can one be so fortunate to make in so short a time?

My hotel bedroom, whilst not unfriendly, lacked the warm, intimate welcome smell of home. I ruffled up the bed to take away its 'snooty' look, and lay down. But sleep didn't come easily after the excitement of the evening. Its shadowy figure crept up on me unexpectedly and I was suddenly awakened by the insistent clamour of a bell,

"Ding, dong. Ding, ding, dong".

I rubbed the sleep from my eyes. It was the market bell! It came from that direction and it meant business was about to begin! The sale bell! It took only seconds to strap on my kilt and slip into my brogues, and, a minute later, I was sprinting up the street, my heart pounding.

Only to find that all was strangely quiet at the market. A solitary, white-coated figure greeted me.

"My, but you are the early one!" In casual tones I murmured, "I thought I heard a bell".

"Did you now? That would be for the chapel".

I made my way to Stoirm's pen. He got up and snuffed me thoughtfully. I unplaited his tail and brushed it out into a beautiful tassel. Gradually the others drifted in to do up their charges. A cheery word here, a wave of hand there. I had that comfortable feeling of belonging. The drinking pails and feeding bins clattered and brushes worked tirelessly.

In time the sale bell rang and I winced when I heard it.

The first bulls were already heading for the arena and Stoirm and I joined them. Through the relay system the auctioneer's voice reached us as if from outer space and we knew the first bull was already pounding the sawdust.

Soon we were waiting in the wings, the next to go in. The yardsman took both our names. The big doors swung open and a sea of faces followed us round and round. Stoirm and I tried so hard not to look like new boys.

"Outwintered this one. Never been inside".

The auctioneer's voice was busy. He got a bid and was off. I thought too much of Stoirm to tally the mounting guineas and felt the final smack of the hammer cut for ever the strings that bound us together. Back at the pen the new owner was waiting. Stoirm was reluctant to be loaded so I stepped forward and lifted one forefoot on to the ramp.

"You fortunate bull," I whispered huskily in his ear. "A big hill farm in the west, with lots of lovely females," and reaching down, I caught his tail and gave it a friendly tug.

Stoirm bounded up into the float and away out of my life, leaving behind in my outstretched hand, a wisp of his titian tassel.

11

For me, every new day develops a pattern of its own as it goes along. One hot day we were hammering in fence posts. Irralee was doing the holding (with a faith I could never hope to emulate) and I was wielding the big hammer.

We paused for a moment to draw breath and a butterfly flitted gracefully around, lit gently on my hand and then, to our astonishment, began to sip the perspiration on my palm. I didn't want to disturb the beautiful creature so we had a longer break than usual and, anyway, who wants to knock in posts on a broiling August day? But that butterfly stayed with us and when we made our tracks for home, followed us.

I felt that this was some blithe spirit I had met somewhere, sometime before, and that he, or she, could join the other butterflies who find a cosy corner in the Croft Douglas ceiling to spend all winter peacefully asleep, awaiting the warm sun of another summer. Little do they know, as they slumber with folded wings, of the elaborate system that Irralee has devised to defeat the stealthy approach of the big spider that fancies a butterfly for a titbit, and how he is swiftly captured and bundled, unceremoniously outside.

I have always had strong feelings about reincarnation and when the large moth flutters wildly at the lighted window as the evening bows to darkness, I can see the face and the anxious expression that spells out the fear of the coming frost and a cold death before morning. So the window is open as a gateway to shelter and the big moth joins the tomtit roosting peacefully, like a feathered powderpuff on the set of antlers in the hall. He, too, knew that the seed or two in his crop — all he could find to eat that day — would never generate sufficient warmth to fend off the icy grip that would come with the night. And the blackbird who knows all about the morse code and hammers out an S.O.S. on the window pane. Where have I met him before? His bright, black eyes say,

"You should know."

A day in June changed my whole way of life, and the sparkle of the dawn set the touch paper of the explosive part of my nature smouldering, with a glow that was soon to send me hurtling across the sky to far away places. It all started when I presented the first of the Vale of Atholl Pipe Band's fund-raising open air Highland Nights. As I looked out over the sea of faces I knew just how the fawn felt when it had stared into the eyes of the murderous pine marten and I shared the thoughts of the fledgling as the moment came to make an uncertain flutter from the warmth and security of the nest.

I took a deep breath and, hoping the microphone would not betray the wild beating of my heart, made my debut as a Highland entertainer. I knew it had been a success as the thunderous applause echoed and re-echoed among the hills. There was an avalanche of appreciation, countless programmes and autograph books to be signed and, occasionally the odd incident that brought me back to earth.

This happened on one of the bigger days when I was presenting the Duke of Atholl and his world famous private army at their Annual Review at Blair Castle. It was always with a great sense of relief that I watched the clouds of black smoke, belched out by the Atholl gunners' cannons, gradually clear to reveal that all was well and not, as my imagination would have it, that the mountain guns had carved a line of mangled bodies through the gathering of humanity and I would be left to explain it all away. But a musical tinkling in the background proved that the castle windows had failed to withstand the blast. The lone piper playing from the battlements made a fitting finale.

The following winter, flighting in with the feathered migrants from Scandinavia, came recognition from abroad with an invitation to the band and myself, as president, to entertain in Copenhagen. Most of the band members (including our two piping daughters) were about to experience their first taste of flying. The airport reminded me of a beehive in full production.

Our flight, it transpired, would be delayed and a meal was provided to mop up the waiting period. I had a fleeting thought that this must be playing havoc with the timing of Irralee's special take off and landing prayers. She has always harboured a mistrust of aeroplanes, but as far as I was concerned there was just time to see that everyone was fed before counting the last one into the plane.

I left the rest to the blond Icelandair hostesses, who had the time of their lives deciding whether safety belts should be worn over or under the sporrans. It was time to relax and look leisurely out of the windows. This was not flying as I knew it, more like a train ride across the fleecy clouds in a land where the sun always shone.

The lady sitting next to me confided that if there was a blanket of cloud below she didn't dare to look out as this brought on a compulsive urge to get out and walk across! She also told me she was a teacher and returning from a holiday in Scotland.

"Oh," I said, "you must be Danish."

171

"I," she said, drawing herself up to full sitting position, "am an Icelander."

Goodness, I thought, do they have those problems in Scandinavia, too? Then came a 'clonk' as the landing gear came down and I overheard one piper say to another,

"What was that?"

To which his companion replied, equally fearfully,

"I think we just hit some fence posts."

The Icelander grabbed my arm and murmured apologetically,

"This is the bit I do not like," but we landed softly and safely in wonderful Copenhagen. Here, an elegant coach swept us up as we emerged from the plane, saw us swiftly through Customs, raced into the city and deposited us at the gates of the heavily guarded Rosenburg Castle, where we were to stay as guests of the Royal Life Guards.

"But first," said the young officer who had been our guide during the coach journey, "I will take you to see the Banan."

I have always tried to to meet a new experience with calm but, on this occasion, I had to draw a deep breath. Covering the wall of the Banan's office was a vividly coloured picture of a huge gorilla with bared fangs, bloodshot eyes and arms and legs like the trunks of massive trees, with a caption in big, black letters, "I am the boss." Beneath this sat a large hunk of manhood, resplendent in Royal Life Guard uniform. He rose like a mountain that had suddenly tired of sitting in the one spot, and the golden tassel dangling from the front of his hat danced merrily as he greeted me. I watched my hand disappear into his massive range of knuckles and miraculously return unharmed and I listened to his comforting words,

"Any problems, any problems at all, just you come to me."

How soon I was to remember them.

"Yens" boomed the Banan. "Conduct our guests to the Mess for some Danish hospitality."

The young officer jumped to attention and led the way. There was a scraping of chairs as the off-duty officers rose to greet us. They had just finished their turn of guarding the Danish crown jewels and soon all was pleasant chatter, punctuated with the clink of glasses as we tasted the national drink, Akvavit, which I learnt meant the same as uisge-beatha — the water of life.

After a few moments the Banan joined us and, in an unthinking moment I asked him,

"Why do they call you the Banan?" and why, oh why, does a silence always fall at a moment like this! The Banan's left eyebrow shot up and the guardsmen were falling about laughing their heads off. A horrible thought struck me. Was it possible he didn't know of his nickname?

The young officer, Yens, hastened to draw me aside and explained, laughingly, that the big officer's favourite expression, when pouring scorn on the heads of drilling recruits, was to liken them to a bunch of bananas. I had with me a bottle of fine malt whisky for just such a moment as this and I pressed it into the hands of the Banan.

To say things went with a bang would be an understatement of the whole trip. Our biggest and broadest piper, in a carefree stride, mistook a glassplate window for an open doorway. The exploding glass ripped him savagely from the knee to thigh and blood spouted from the gash with horrific abandon. The Pipe Sergeant and I quickly set about staunching the flow.

"It's bad," the sergeant muttered — that was exactly

what I was thinking, and where was the Banan?

He appeared from nowhere, floating above me like a cross between a giant genie and a guardian angel. Looking up, I said,

"I have a problem," and The Banan went into action. The medical officer was summoned and appeared in an instant. Seconds later we were on board a military ambulance, screaming our way through the streets of the city to Copenhagen Royal Infirmary, our piper receiving royal treatment. The Danish nurses fussed around the tartan and hairy knees, which caused quite a flutter. I had a word with the surgeon who was scrutinising the final stitches.

"This man," he said, "must rest for at least a week.

"Ah'm playin' the morn," muttered the big piper dourly.

"What does he say?" inquired the surgeon.

"He wants to play in the big parade tomorrow," I explained.

"Do you realise," the surgeon's English was faultless and precise, "that any undue strain put upon this leg could reopen the wound with a loss of blood that would be more than serious?"

"Ah'm playin' the morn," the big piper's tones were more determined than ever. The surgeon turned on his heel and allowed himself two words,

"Mad, mad!" and departed.

Next morning the reveille bugle held an urgent and excited note, and the rising sun smiled down on the parade of Scottish tartan bordered by the red, blue and silver of the Danish Life Guards. Then came the command to march. The pipes and drums took the morning apart and sent the castle pigeons rocketing skywards.

Those Danish stitches must have been really strong, as

they took the stomp of the big piper's foot from Rosenburg, all the way up the famous Walking Street and into Copenhagen's magnificent Main Square, there to march and countermarch in the blazing sunshine. And the mass of mankind who had come to watch and listen moved with us like a tidal wave. And flow they did, a mass of bodies that swept us back to Rosenburg Castle and, in that moment the Life Guards really proved that they did save lives by closing the enormous gates against the multitude! At dawn the next day the call of the bugle sent out the sobbing note of farewell.

The Banan, marking his approval as only he could with the gesture of bestowing the supreme accolade, pinned to each side of my doublet collar the badge of the Royal Life Guards and, to a place just above my heart, the coveted gold insignia of a Life Guard's officer. We hugged each other wordlessly.

As I counted the pipers and drummers onto the plane I thought what a fitting climax it seemed. But at that moment I was handed, by special messenger, an invitation from the St. Andrew's Society of Denmark to be their guest of honour at their January Burns' supper and knew then I would return.

12

It seemed no time at all before I was once again making my way to Denmark, but this time aboard the *Winston Churchill,* leaving a foam flecked path through the stormy North Sea. It was night, and late, but sleep did not come easily. I gazed through the port-hole in my cabin and watched in awe as the rolling seas revelled in the torment of the ship's passing. The moon lit the scene in a cold, dispassionate light and relentlessly leaned down and licked the crest of each new wave with her silvery tongue.

We docked at Esjberg next morning and continued the journey overland and oversea by train, and made the discovery that, in this land, trains, too, travel across the water. We stopped at Odense, where they make marzipan and at Århus, which is the target for jokes by other Danes such as, having their wipers on the inside of their windscreens so they can breathe heavily with a woosh-woosh-woosh. This is sufficient to make any Dane dissolve in laughter (except those from Århus).

All journeys, like life, come to a turning or an end and I was met in Copenhagen by the President of the St. Andrew's Society who took me to my hotel. It was at one corner of the Main Square which already held many memories. The next morning I spent sight-seeing. First, to the Mermaid; how small and dainty compared to the picture described by Hans Anderson. But, not far away, was something really breathtaking. A huge statue of a woman, who came alive as you watched, holding the shaft of a plough with one hand while the other, with a cruel whip, mercilessly lashed four harnessed bulls. How the animals baukled, jibbed and strained at their task, their lathered flanks atwitch with torture and, from their nostrils flew a fine spray, tinged with red.

As I stared, a lady tugged the sleeve of my jacket and put my mind at rest by explaining that the fountain water leading to the bulls' nostrils was purposefully tinted. She asked if she might take my photograph and, by way of return, told me the story of the statue.

It depicted a lady who was given permission, by the king of Denmark, to claim as much land as she could plough in one night. She was no lady, but a witch, who changed her four sons into bulls and, lashing them to the point of exhaustion, claimed the whole of Zeeland.

Onwards, I wandered through the streets of this wonderful city. A tantalising smell drifted to my nostrils from the open doorway of a restaurant. The windows were draped in tartan and, above the entrance, in big letters unbelievably, THE KILT.

Inside I found a young man dressed in spotless white. His right eyebrow reached up to tilt his chef's hat to an even more precarious angle.

"What to eat?" he inquired, politely.

I pointed to a mound of newly-cut steaks. The chef deftly speared one, tossed it in the air and it landed with a sizzling sigh on the hot plate in the corner. In that moment I was reminded that, as yet, I had no idea what the content of my speech was to hold for tonight. Between mouthfuls, I scribbled furiously on the multi-coloured 'Kilt' serviette before me.

What, I wrote, did Burns do to bring us all together in a land, far removed from his birth, to celebrate his birthday one hundred and eighty odd years after he had died? I think he taught us how to speak to a flower, how to share and understand the trials and tribulations of a field mouse. He taught us that the supreme force in the world is Love, the love of a boy for a girl, the love of a man for his fellowman, the love for the country of our birth.

We have a modern song "I want to teach the world to sing". Burns taught the world to sing nearly two centuries ago, with a song that still echoes round the world and plays havoc with the heart strings at the moment of parting.

"Should auld acquaintance be forgot
And never brought to mind?
Should auld acquaintance be forgot,
And days o' lang syne?"

I sighed contentedly. The steak was delicious and I now knew what I was going to say that night. A lady with a tartan plaid draped from her left shoulder, appeared as from nowhere.

"You are the first 'real kilt' we ever have".

I was trying to think of an answer when she continued,

"If you tell me what you wear underneath, there is nothing to pay".

I absorbed the shock of this statement by glancing at the bill now resting alongside my plate. Steak appeared to be a very expensive commodity in Copenhagen, but it occurred to me that I had not yet uttered a word since entering The Kilt, so I looked into her eyes and told her how deep, dark and brown they were. She pondered this for only a moment then, without the flutter of an eyelash, said,

"Ah, that's how it is! There is nothing to pay."

"Beannaich leibh", I said to her, and completely forgot the part I was playing, explained confidentially, 'it means 'Blessing with you'."

Madame was overcome, but not quite. The photographer was there and waited to take my picture in

179

the doorway.

I bounced gaily into the sunshine, past a crowd of people waiting patiently at the kerbside and skipped deftly in between the cars, finally to cross the street straight into the arms of a policeman, who surveyed me sadly, unbuttoned the top pocket of his tunic and brought out a little book. At the same time he told me that it was an offence to cross against the red light and carried the penalty of a fine.

I gazed at him with my very best blank expression and thought I would 'try it' once again. Irralee, who was sent at a tender age to Harris to learn the very essence of Gaelic, maintains that my efforts are the worst in Perthshire. But I thought this Danish policeman wouldn't know any better. He didn't, and stared at me in astonishment, pushing his hat back as if to ease some sudden pressure on his brow.

At that moment, a police patrol car slid smoothly alongside. I knew it was a police car as the first four letters were right and it had a revolving, flashing light. The window of the car slid down and revealed a pair of twinkling eyes over a military moustache that swept a path for flashing white teeth and I listened, only half believing, to the voice.

"Hello, Gideon. Jump in!"

By this time we were surrounded by a crowd of interested spectators, who watched silently as I was taken into custody, but waved enthusiastically as I waved a carefree farewell.

My rescuer swept the car at high speed through a maze of city traffic and yet, miraculously, managed to carry on a flow of conversation with a voice that crackled from the dashboard. I watched, listened, and admired. The object of my admiration said in a quick aside,

"You do not remember me?" I was a Royal Life

Guards officer when you were in the Rosenburg Barracks last year. I am just going off duty and will take you to see the Banan".

We screeched up to the Rosenburg gates where a crested Official Card saw us through the crossed bayonets. The Banan was there, seated under the portrait of his gorilla. The caption, too, was still bold and clear, "I AM THE BOSS". He was just as I remembered him. He remembered me, too, and embraced me in a bonecrushing hug.

"Gaidyin", he had a way of saying my name in the best Scottish Doric. The golden tassle on his hat danced with joy as he shepherded me to the Officers' Mess.

"Akvavit!" he ordered. "Akvavit for this meeting".

The Banan pointed to the window. "Remember when your piper, Sam, walked through it?"

I remembered all right. He pointed to the gilt inscription above saying SAMS DOOR and his gigantic frame shook with spasms of uncontrollable laughter. I really appreciated the Danes' deep sense of humour.

"Gaidyin", the Banan was serious now. "You are just in time to come with me while I see to the Changing of the Guard at the Queen's Palace".

It was a splendid affair, with stamping horses, mechanically moving men, mixed with the condiments of pomp and pageantry. There was drama, too. The new Guard came forward, each toe following the heel in front in the inch-perfect precision for which the Danish Guards are famous, when the leader halted just a fraction too soon . . .!

They were the Banan's latest recruits and I heard him moan in an agony all of his own,

"It's a 'shunting train'," and, sure enough at the sudden stop of the leader the rest went, 'bump, bump, bump' into each other, like so many carriages. But the watching crowd applauded enthusiastically, thinking it was part of the plan.

The Danish Queen appeared and presented a glass of wine to the Officer who was 'taking care' for the night. The Banan mopped his brow and, in the process, seemed to instil a memo or two. He drove me back to my hotel with the driving wheel delicately poised in his right hand while he answered calls on his telephone with his left. I had never ridden in a car with telephone facilities before, but believed that anything with the Banan in charge, was possible. He turned to me and said,

"I hear you are to be at the Langoline, the Royal Yachting Pavilion, tonight. The Queen could be there, too. She likes to come unnoticed, just like her shopping trips to the city".

The Banan was right. The Burns' Night promised, right from the start, to be a 'right royal' affair, with everyone, who seemed to be someone, there.

The Danes, in my experience, besides having a profound sense of humour, love to eat and drink and, perhaps most of all, to dress up. This night was certainly one they had earmarked for something special.

The British Tourist Authority were recording my toast to the Immortal Memory and had also thought it fit and proper that I should have an escort. She spoke, I was told, at least half a dozen languages. But, when we met outside the imposing Langoline, she didn't need to speak. She wore a long, white, satin evening gown and a small glinting tiara on her blonde head. Her hair flowed in a golden cascade all the way down to where she sat down.

A Major of the Royal Danish Guards, resplendent in full dress uniform, toasted the British Queen and the British Ambassador toasted the Danish Queen. The clinking kiss of glasses was prelude to the sips that set the seal on the solemnity of protocol.

I was next, the guest of honour. I have always wondered why, in moments like these, the butterflies, that have been peacefully slumbering inside me, suddenly decide to awaken, spread their wings and flutter around. When I opened my mouth to speak it was with the fervent prayer that none of them would fly out. But, I tell myself, if you have something to say, say it from the heart. And, all the time, the B.T.A. recorder was sitting with a long, circular, tongue that lapped up every sound and every word.

When you have given of your best, it is a good thing to savour the sweet sound of appreciation, and when it is continued and sustained, it is a wine that goes straight to the head. It made me enjoy, all the more, my plate of haggis, bashed turnips and mashed potatoes.

On my right, sat a bearded gentleman who wore a silver cross on a scarlet ribbon, that spoke of the highest accolade. He was the nearest, in my mind, to a real Viking, as he balanced a plate in his left hand and, with his right, deftly scooped out the centre of the haggis and filled the gap with whisky, then, as a builder mixes cement, patted and cajoled it into a smooth mixture. I have never seen a dish supped with such relish.

"You like the haggis?" I ventured. His features formed themselves into a display of sheer ecstacy,

"It is good. It is good", he said. "But, oh, the gravy, the gravy!"

It was an evening to be remembered. I thanked my escort, called a taxi and bade her good-night. It felt good to be outside in the fresh air. It was cool, so cool, and the sky over the water nursed a star that winked and blinked, and wanted to say something. I was still watching that star when a car slid alongside and a taximan spoke softly, and haltingly,

"You wish to go somewhere?"

I knew where I should go — back to my hotel to take off the finery of lace and velvet and rest to face the happenings of tomorrow. But, at the end of occasions like this I always feel like a clock that has been well and truly wound up and requires time to run down before rest comes.

"Yes", I said, "take me where the action is".

The taximan beamed.

"For you", he purred, "it has to be The Ka Ka du."

"Is it not too late?" I flung the question, half hoping he would call the whole thing off, but the taximan was made of sterner stuff.

"Not to worry", he said, "this place does not open until after midnight". And, so saying, he drove me through the city of a million lights to a quieter side street where we stopped underneath a row of flaming torches. The smoking tips of their tapered tongues licked upwards towards a galaxy of coloured neon lights which worked overtime to keep alive the form of a giant cockatoo.

"This," I asked in awed tone, "is the place?"

"This", replied the taximan, with the reverence of a minister at the end of a lengthy sermon, "is, truly, the place".

A fatherly gentleman, immaculate in evening dress, appeared in the doorway, bowed and led me inside, where a dark haired, attractive girl helped herself to my coat.

"Just one moment please!"

A soft, but compelling, arm wound its way around me. But it was only a temporary delay, as her friend, in the opposite row of cloaks and coats, took our photograph. Before I was released the coat girl whispered in my ear,

"I tell you this, because I like you, watch out for the

ones with cash register eyes".

I winked, solemnly and discreetly, as if
acknowledging a message from MI5. The barmaid, after
greeting me with a saucy look, found her voice,

"For you, an Elephant Beer," and she giggled
hilariously to herself.

I looked around. I had never seen so many girls who
had spent so much to clothe themselves in so little.

"Why", the barmaid giggled again, "do you not go
upstairs, there is Cabaret there and the Italian Ladies'
Band."

I floated effortlessly up the stairs. The Italian Ladies
were playing softly for couples who were dancing.
Although the lights were very subdued the leader
spotted me immediately and switched the melody to a
rendering of 'Loch Lomond'. I made my way towards
the musicians, like a mouse who had sipped the antidote
to fear and faces up to the cats.

A delicate hand, decorated with what seemed to be
'top weight' in rings and bracelets, also held a
microphone, and a sun-drenched voice said,

"Will you sing?"

And sing I did! "By yon bonnie banks, And by yon
bonnie braes" and all the world-wide Harry Lauder
favourite songs. The Italian Ladies strained every sequin
in their skintight evening dresses to follow me. I was just
bowing out when two girls bounced onto the stage,
wearing Stetson hats, gun belts, high -heeled boots and
spurs and nothing else that I could notice.

They started to sing one of my favourites, The Red
River Valley. The moment was too much for me. I
jumped back onto the stage and, linking arms with the
girls, joined in their song and they, in turn, crooned
in harmony as I delivered the Gaelic verses. There is no
greater appreciation than that for the spontaneous

moment but I decided that it was time, when they were chanting for more, to go home.

"So soon?" the dark haired girl helped me on with my coat. "I heard you sing. You were very good".

The fatherly gentleman at the door waved a beckoning hand into the night and, from nowhere, my transport to sanctuary appeared under the flickering torchlight.

Next morning, I ordered porridge for breakfast. It took a long time coming, but someone in the kitchen was doing a lot of homework to produce the correct dish. A large bowl of steaming porridge, a smaller one of creamy milk and a dish of salt were set before me by the largest piece of Danish femininity I had so far seen. She stood behind me and watched closely while I supped. I finished it all — I had to! I knew the Great Dame behind wasn't going to let me away before I had supped every drop. It was a formidable bowl, but I stuck to it for Scotland's sake, when the manager appeared at my side with a large menu card in his hand that looked, to me, like a flag of truce.

"Your car is outside. It is urgent".

I doubted my ability to rise but made the effort and my way to the door. The British Tourist Association had arranged everything. The car was there, engine ticking over and the B.T.A. manager was there to tell me that the recording made at The Supper last night had been edited and was part of a programme to go out from Copenhagen Radio and TV Station that morning. I, too, was expected to appear in person. As I entered the studio the manager whispered,

"When you are asked about the Scottish Highlands, tell them!"

So I did and, for good measure, sang "The Road to the Isles". It must have pleased them as they treated me to a sumptuous lunch at the famous Oskar Davidsen's, where it states, on the yard long menu, that condemned prisoners had selected this restaurant for their last meal.

In the afternoon there was a meeting with the Press, the highlight being an interview with Copenhagen's top lady columnist.

"Tell me," she said, "what do you do in Copenhagen at the end of the day, when you have finished selling Scotland?"

It was one of those times when a reply is made without due thought.

"Oh," I answered, "I go to the Kakadu."

My questioner's eyebrows shot up to register the ultimate in surprise.

"Really", she said, and selected her next words as if she were popping bullets into a revolver. "What do you think of the lovely ladies there?"

With caution now thrown entirely to the winds I replied,

"Well, it makes a change from looking into the eyes of Highland heifers!"

The next morning heralded the last day of my stay. It also brought the crop of newspapers. The "Politiken" and the lady journalist had really 'gone to town' and given over a page to myself. My face grinned cheerfully back at me, even when it came to the Kakadu and the Highland heifers.

At the B.T.A. Offices in Mountegade, I was briefed on my next yearly visit — to bring a team of pipers and dancers, making a start at Esjberg, two nights at Åarhus, two more at Odense, two at Copenhagen, finishing up with a dash, on my own, on the flying boat across to Sweden and Malmo. All details were finalised and I had the afternoon to myself.

I decided to have another look around the city I was

learning to love. But, where to go? Kirsten, my blonde escort for the Big Night drew a plan.

"Here", she said, "are some of the finest old buildings of the city, but do not go further down to this part of the waterfront". She stabbed the offending district with the point of her pencil.

I promised, with my hand on my heart, to follow her instructions, but my wandering footsteps, and a burning curiosity, took me to just that place down by the waterfront. A bright young thing, with a bright coloured bandana around her head and wearing a pair of short, blue velvet, pants, fell into step beside me and inquired,

"Are you real?"

"I hope so", I replied. "I didn't see my name in today's Deaths".

This remark was entirely lost on her. She pointed to my badger sporran.

"What's in there?"

"My money."

"Can I put some in?"

I stared, unbelievingly, into those pale blue eyes while she fumbled in a velvet pocket and produced two Danish crowns. Lifting the badger's snout she solemnly dropped them down its throat.

"It's for luck", she said. I have been told to do this if I see a real Scotsman".

I thought for just a moment, dipped into the badger and gave the girl a ten kroner note.

"That", I said, "is your first piece of luck".

She smiled, a young 'starting out in the world' smile.

"Where do you go now?"

"Where do I get a lager?"

She pointed across the street. There was a brilliantly lit window with the name 'Tattoo Jake' and, to the left, a dingy sign displaying a huge bottle with its neck pointing down a short flight of stairs, and yet another sign, set at a tipsy angle, 'The Captain's Cabin'. She ran after me as I crossed the street.

"There are bad men in there, who will rob you".

"What!" I said. "In broad daylight!"

"It happens, even in the sunlight".

At that moment, I could easily have been afraid but wasn't going to let this slip of a girl witness it. A hairy face stared at me through a port hole in the door for just a second, before it slowly creaked open and admitted me. After the sunlit street my eyes took their own time to note the sawdust sprinkled floor, the barrels which served as tables and the bottles with their flickering candles.

To my left, a dwarf, with a little body and a huge head topped off with a seaman's hat, sat on a high stool, dangling his chubby legs. He was talking excitedly to an enormous seaman, whose magnificent chest had the stitches of his jersey screaming in agony. On my right, a swarthy type, who could only be described as in the cut throat class, was making an impassioned plea to a painted lady, coolly smoking a huge cigar. And, in front of me, a sight to make my mother's heart bleed — a young Eskimo girl sprawled helplessly over a barrel top, her hand still clutching an empty bottle. Seated on a beer crate against the far wall, with his eyes firmly fixed on the battered beams of the ceiling, an accordionist squeezed out the haunting melody which, I thought only ran through my head.

I made my way uncertainly to an unoccupied barrel and seated myself. Another hunk of a man loomed up, swept a match across the surface of the barrel and lit the candle in the bottle. I knew it to be the Danish sign of a welcome. The big man was the landlord and his voice like the roar of the sea.

"Tuborg?"

"Yes, please", and deftly, he flipped the top off the bottle and spun it through the air to clink into a copper bucket. I could tell they had done it before, he and the copper bucket.

"Three kroner". The money disappeared into a sporran-like purse under an apron stiff with beer stains. I nodded towards the Eskimo girl's still form.

"She has come from Greenland for her education", the landlord rumbled. I searched for a reply, but could not find one. I couldn't find a glass, either, then realised why a glass in these surroundings would be dangerous. So, I took a sip from the bottle and was about to take another when a figure loomed up in front of me and, in a mixture of German and broken English, asked, to 'look at my knife'.

I thought it best to humour him and laid it in the palm of his hand. The blade shone in the candlelight, the silver blinked and the cairngorm glowed with a cold confidence, which I did not feel. It was my dress sgian dhubh and, with a snatch, I retrieved it. The figure turned round and disappeared, but only for a moment. He was back again with an oily, green, package which he slid towards me 'for the knife'.

I pushed it back, without examination. 'No thanks''. But back came the oily package again. This time each word held its full measure of menace.

"For — the — knife".

The dwarf's chubby legs stopped swinging, a smoke ring from the painted lady's cigar hung motionless in the air, the accordionist sobbed only notes of sadness, and I had the feeling that everyone was listening, even the Eskimo girl. I took a deep breath and expelled it in one word,

"NO".

Two eyes glinted cruelly above me and the voice said, "Then I take it", and, seizing the bottle with its candle still stuck fast, he swung it aloft. I watched the inverted flame lick greedily at the hairs on his arm and the hot tallow trickle down towards his wrist. I didn't have time to feel afraid, but gazed in fascination as a bulging, vividly coloured arm appeared from behind and snaked its way across my assailant's throat. The picture that clearly stood out was a lady having a bath in a glass of wine! Even at this moment of crisis I thought, that if this were a sample of Tattoo Jake's work, he was indeed an artist.

A quick jerk which almost tipped the lady out of her glass, and the bottle crashed to the floor. I smelt the smoking candle and the singeing hair and watched the arm, with the lady in the glass, haul the body, heels dragging, across the floor to disappear down a hatch which had suddenly, and conveniently, been opened.

After some muffled thumps and bumps the landlord, owner of the tattoed arm, reappeared, kicked the hatch top which banged noisily into place and stared hard at the accordionist, who resumed playing. I really needed a drink and ordered two ice-cold Akvavit, pushed one towards mine host and we drank together.

"Skol!".

I rose, shook the hand at the end of the tattooed arm and made for the door. I looked back once, in time to see the Eskimo girl roll her raven locks to one side and open an almond eye.

My evening had been planned for me, I had to speak at the English Debating Club. It said at the heading of their letter, founded 5th November, 1885 and gave a list of the past speakers. The list was impressive, with the titles, accolades and letters, which queued up to follow their names!

THE KILT FOR KEEPS

I had been billed as, simply,
"An hour with Gideon. A true Scot."
I had, indeed, to speak for one hour in one of
Copenhagen's biggest hotels, The Scandinavia. The
people were there, sitting in a hushed, polite
expectancy. The rostrum was there, too, with a
concealed light for notes. I didn't have any. There were
notices everywhere, "Please speak English", that was
my cue. So I began,
"As notified, I am going to speak to you in English".
The hour I had been allotted melted away, like an ice
cube in a hot sun, and finished with five minutes of
question time. The questions were many and varied, but
the final one came out of the blue and from a lady who, I
thought, looked to belong to the Sisters of Mercy. But
she didn't.
"It says here", and she waved the evening's
programme" that you are a true Scot. Well, are you?"
My brain, like a well-kept pistol was ready and
pointed.
"Madam", I said coolly, "that is to be the subject of
next year's English Debate".
I had time only for a cup of tea and a Danish pastie
when another taxi took me to the SPORVEJENES
ENGELSK KLUB. For a living, the members took care
of Copenhagen's huge and intricate network of
transport. The Klub was packed. My task here was to
provide the commentary through a film of the wild life of
the Scottish Highlands.
In spite of not seeing it before, the words came easily
to my mouth with the sight of scenery I knew well: the
lochs reflecting every mood of the heather-clad hills; the
red grouse, the blackcock, the capercailzie and the
spellbinding dives of the osprey.
At the finish of the film, I entertained with the help of

193

an excellent Danish accordionist and the appreciation was unstinted. A lady rose, as I thought to give the 'hearty vote of thanks'. I was wrong.

She spoke, she said, on behalf of all the ladies present who would like to know if I put on anything under my kilt! Remembering my reply at the Hotel Scandinavia, I said, amidst a burst of cheering,

"That, ladies, is the subject of my film talk for next year".

Back at my hotel the hands of the clock were pointing to midnight and my two selves were engaged in a wrestling match. The 'good' one, for once, looked like being a winner and said, "You are tired and will have to be up to make the long trip home". But the other self sneered, "Are you a man? This is your last night in Wonderful Copenhagen and you wish to spend it asleep!" There was no answer. I was outside hailing a taxi.

"Where to?"

"The Kakadu".

The fatherly gentleman in the doorway greeted me as if I were his only son.

"The Big Boss wants to see you", and he conducted me upstairs. The Big Boss was there and threw himself upon me with something between a bear hug and a stranglehold.

"Never", he gasped, "never, never, do we have such advertising. Tonight you, my kilted friend, are my guest. Everything, for you, is on the house", and he piloted me to a tastefully set table, lit with soft, flickering, candle light.

We started with Russian caviar. It was my first taste of the genuine article and I gulped as I calculated the cost of each forkful but, nevertheless, found time to notice it was delicious. We were just washing down the roast pheasant with a superb white wine when my host rose and excused himself.

"Urgent business in town", and, at his bidding, a girl flowed out of the darkness. "This is Jetta. She will look after you".

I shook hands with the Big Boss, then turned to look at my new companion. She moved towards me, a lithe, young, tigress, her muscles coupled together with sensuous sinews, and the minimum of flesh flowed effortlessly in rhythmic ripples under the silken skin of her dress. Settling on a chair opposite me, as lightly as a piece of thistledown, she gazed directly into my eyes, parted her lips slightly and her lips glistened to match the glitter in her eyes.

What do you do when you come face to face with a hungry looking tigress? Of course, you feed it! I signalled a waiter to bring her a generous glass of wine, and ordered roast pheasant. She lapped the wine, cat-like, still watching me, then she leaned forward and the whites of her eyes were clear, looking translucent in the candlelight.

"Just say when you want to go upstairs".

In my confusion, I waved away the suggestion. But Jetta was a girl of purpose. She reached across the table and placed her hand on mine. Her voice was gently reassuring.

"It is what the Big Boss has said. I, too, am what you call 'on the house'."

I was as a mouse in her clutches and remembered I had told Irralee, jokingly, before I left home, that, if I 'misbehaved' I would have to buy her another pony. I didn't struggle, but reflected that I had meant to buy her another one, anyway.

Suddenly, I was released. The pheasant had arrived and Jetta set about doing a neat demolition job.

195

"This is 'goot'," she said between mouthfuls and looked across at me again, her eyes dancing mischievously. "I am looking forward to seeing what a real Scotsman wears underneath!"

Inwardly, I groaned, "Oh, no. Not again".

I took a leaf out of the Big Boss's book, looked at my watch and stood up, excusing myself,

"So sorry, I have some urgent business in town".

Jetta stood up, too. She seemed suddenly to have changed and now looked the girl she was. Her voice was charged with sincerity as she said,

"I meet many people. They are like mirrors, some are kinder than others. How I have enjoyed being with you tonight".

We both leant on the table and reached across to kiss, and I went out into the night. I remember that kiss, it tasted of temptation and roast pheasant.

When I said "Urgent business in town", I had really meant it. The answer to the ever-recurring question had suddenly come to me, and my footsteps turned toward the waterfront and Tattoo Jake.

The light was still in his window and Jake was just as I had imagined him; a stocky figure with a pointed silvery beard, seated in a swivel chair and surrounded by rows of lethal looking weapons and electric drills. Jake had the hands of an artist, they were spread out before him awaiting the opportunity to create some fantastic design on a canvas of human skin, and, by his side, truly an incredible hulk of a man with a huge paunch — an avalanche of flesh hanging perilously over a leather belt that strove mightily to contain it and hold up his trousers at the same time. He had to be an enormous man, he had a big responsibility. I could tell at a glance he was Jake's 'Minder'.

I made the first move by pointing to a chart on the wall

and at the picture of a dainty colourful butterfly.

"How much?"

Jake was an artist and allowed the question to fly right over the top of his head, but the 'Minder' gave his paunch a much-needed hitch, cleared his throat and rumbled,

"One hundred kroner".

"The butterfly. I would like there", pointing to the meaty part of my bottom.

Two pairs of eyes switched to each other then back to gaze directly at me. I knew that, without a twitch of a facial muscle, Jake and his 'Minder' were silently 'laughing their heads off', but, in next to no time, I was leaning over Jake's table.

Now, anyone who says this type of operation is not painful has either never experienced it or are lying through their teeth. The needles of Jake's drills drove at a red-hot pace through the tender part of my anatomy and forced me to clench my teeth together in a way that tried to hurt more than the hurt. Meantime, Jake was warming to his work and the 'Minder' never took his eyes off me, seeming to search and seek for the slightest sign of weakness.

In a huge mirror, facing me, I could see Jake at work. His movements were decisive and swift, one might say 'quick on the draw' as his left hand kept snatching at a pile of tissues. I soon saw the object of the exercise. He was mopping up blood, my blood! I consoled myself with the thought that it was a good colour.

Now I knew why the sailors got 'tanked up' before having their sweethearts' names drilled across their chests. I had, I realised, walked into this experience stone, cold, sober, and suffered for it, probably to spend the next day or two eating off the mantlepiece.

At last it was over and Jake gave me a mirror for a

197

quick glance at his handiwork. The butterfly was there all right, but before I had time to appreciate its colouring, it became the reddest of Red Admirals and Jake was slapping pads of cotton wool over and around it.

"Keep the pad on for tonight", growled the 'minder', producing a bottle and three glasses. Then Jake spoke his one and only sentence,

"It is the first time I do a real Scotsman. Skol".

And so we flew home together, the Danish butterfly and I.

Besides pandering to the ponies I try to compensate to Irralee further for sharing life with me, by giving her tea and toast in bed every morning. When I crawl out from under the covers Irralee automatically rolls over onto my side of the bed, which she says, is always far warmer than hers.

It was the second morning of my return from Copenhagen and I was just reaching for my kilt, when Irralee sat bolt upright in bed and inquired in strangled tones,

"What's that?"

"That", I said airily, "is the Danish equivalent of a "By Appointment" Crest. They call it a summerfool".

Irralee wouldn't accept that, so I had to sit down and tell her the whole story — Kakadu — everything. She seemed to have mixed feelings when I came to the bit about the pony, but said,

"Let me have a clear look at it", and was silent for a moment or two.

"It's beautiful", she said, and, pulling the blankets over her head, lay in wait for her tea and toast.

Apart from Irralee's early morning 'viewing' the butterfly remained undiscovered and slumbered peacefully beneath the tartan pleats. That is, until I was called upon to go to Germany and help boost the products that British Wool was putting on display at a big exhibition at Offenburg, a place where the world comes to look, approve and purchase what is on offer.

I have found that work comes first in Germany and starts very early in the morning. So, at the Offenburg Exhibition we started at 8 a.m. and worked our way through the day, and I awoke one morning to find I had completely lost my voice!

I set out, whilst the others were having their breakfast, to find a doctor. I didn't have far to go. At the corner of the street was an impressive building with a huge, highly polished, brass plate that spelt out the message in three different languages — Doctor's Surgery. There was a red, winking light directly underneath, which I pushed, and was almost immediately admitted by a young lady whose features I could barely see for the dazzling whiteness of her uniform.

Language was no problem. Wordlessly, I pointed to my throat and was guided to a large room, with basins of placid porcelain faced up with angular chairs fitted with uninviting headrests and tables that waited at their sides, set with rows of gleaming cutlery that ranged from a fine point to a bayonet.

The doctor had a pointed, black, beard and most professional manner, but I felt, instinctively, that he did not want to converse, his English being just about as good as my German. He raised black, bushy, eyebrows and I pointed, once again, to my throat.

"Do you fume?" he asked.

Ordinarily, I would have thought this quite funny, but I realised he was serious and wanted to know if I smoked. I shook my head. He looked me straight in the eye and opened his mouth. I took his cue and opened mine. Whereupon, he popped what looked like a small telescope in his eye and gazed intently down my throat. He emerged and raised his right arm. In response, a young nurse appeared and piloted me behind a secretive screen.

"Clothes off, bitte", she said.

I knew she had said, please, but I wasn't having any and croaked painfully,

"It's only my throat".

It was to no avail. She held her hand out.

"Your clothes. It is what the doctor has ordered", she said with Germanic finality. So, I surrendered my doublet, and unfastened my kilt. The nurse studied me closely as if she had just seen the dawn of a beautiful day.

"It's a schmetterling", she gasped and remained in a trance while the doctor advanced with a syringe at the ready. He uttered only one word,

"Injection".

The nurse disappeared but returned with all the other nurses who chorused in unison,

"Not on the schmetterling!"

Gallantly, he bowed to his staff and jabbed me on the left buttock. The nurses clapped their hands in the manner their country reserves for moments that are really appreciated, slowly at first gradually increasing in tempo, faster and faster sounding like the release of a hundred homing pigeons. The doctor saw me to the surgery door.

"You Schottish at Exhibition. I have heard. I send pills", and we shook hands, and I smiled my thanks.

Later that day, I was called to the Exhibition First Aid Post and the fair, buxom nurse in charge led me past a neat row of beds to her office. Motioning me in, she closed the door and, from a cabinet, produced a box of pills, selected one and handed it to me and filled a glass with a thick red liquid. I swallowed the pill with the aid of the syrupy-tasting liquid.

"Thank you", I said, delighted to find my voice again.

The nurse looked pleased too, and her cool medical manner melted away as she said, almost shyly,

"May I see the schmetterling, too?"

She dropped to her knees by my side, she even knew the correct side! So for this German nurse, I reached down, caught the pleats of my kilt, and carefully raised the tartan curtain. I didn't look down, but heard her deep, shuddering, sigh,

"Eine Schöne Schmetterling".

13

Sweeping up the lochside, wing tip to wing tip, come the oyster catchers, with just the heart beats from their downy breasts to drive and direct the powerful flight feathers. They are noiseless until they open their orange beaks and cry "Be quick, be quick". It was they, the story goes, who saw the searching soldiers, with orders to slay all newborn boys, and swooped low over the maidens who were hiding the baby Moses in the bullrushes, screaming, "Be quick, be quick".

The oyster catchers remind me, too, that April is here and it is time to sow the crops we have planned through the dark nights of winter. The field chosen for hay is already rippling to the stroking of the breeze. The broody hens are turning their eggs with a contented shuffle, crooning over their clutch of gems which they wouldn't swap for all the unhatchable diamonds, rubies and pearls. Very soon the chicks will be urgently tapping their way into the outside world and there will be an element of surprise for the hens sitting on the duck and goose eggs!

The Highland cows are, one by one, drifting away to their favourite, secluded, calving places, and the fat-bellied mare will soon have the company of her long-legged foal.

Before the swallows fly in, this year's spate of visitors will be arriving and it will be time to give the haggis its sacrificial rites before the fascinated tourists and introduce them to the delights of the ceilidh.

Then the incoming cuckoo (I find it hard to like this

bird) will tell us it is May and the native birds will be in full song. The dunnock in the hedge will sit tightly on her ever-so-blue eggs; the honey bee will plunder the colourful clusters of apple blossom; baby rabbits will be everywhere, popping up and down, and in and out, in wide-eyed surprise at their new found freedom as their mothers, with other things to think about, prepare yet another nest for yet another family; and the evening entertainments are, like the weather, 'hotting up'.

The open air Highland Nights will be in full swing and, as the evening approaches, I study my watch and cast an anxious eye at the sky.

July means its time to make the hay and, at the first hint of settled weather, it's off with everything, bar the kilt, and into the hay-cutting in the blazing sunshine. The scythe will swing and the tall grass fall with a sigh; the bees solve their overcrowding problem by swarming; the baby swallows peek over the edge of their nest; the young rabbits will be almost three-quarters grown and, fortunately, will have lost that cuddly, baby look. They will then be at their best for the stew-pot, so it hurt so much to take one, especially if he is a garden marauder!

The garden will proudly present the first young carrots, parsnips, turnips and spring onions (they make the rabbit stew delicious) and, together with the new potatoes, a knob of butter, and a sprig of wild mint, makes a feast fit for a king. There is the deep satisfaction that it has all been produced by our own effort, on our own land. But not entirely, for 'it is fed and watered . . . .'.

August, I think, belies its name. It is a magic month. The year is at its prime and proud in maturity. The hill air is heavy with the scent of heather and bogmyrtle.

The red grouse on the moors will take come catching on the twelfth; the big stag, with the shine of a good

summer's grazing on his coat, will find time to gaze into the still waters of a mountain tarn and, seeing the flowing mane and mighty antlers, roar at his own reflection.

In the fields the mushrooms are indulging in their annual, bionic upsurge, to burst through the surface of the earth with beads of early morning dew glistening on their foreheads. We believe, that, like the free-range egg, the wild mushroom holds the real goodness. The maggots share this belief and we race to gather them before the maggots strike. The bulk of the basketfuls are preserved and the remaining 'buttons' go towards brightening up the breakfast bacon and eggs.

The great 'horse' mushrooms, as big as dinnerplates, are fried gently in butter and, with a sprinkle of salt and a liberal dash of black pepper, are a steak in themselves.

September and October invariably go hand in hand and together tint the leaves, vying with each other's lights and shades until, under their efforts, the whole countryside revels in a blaze of colour.

Long-billed, soft-feeding woodcock fly in from Scandinavia; the last big run of salmon is on and, if you don't catch one now, you never will. The pink salmon cutlets, simmering in the salted water, are allowed to cool back, undisturbed, in their own juice, then flaked out onto a bed of fresh lettuce from the garden and surrounded by the sweet smell that belongs only to the newly-picked tomatoes which Irralee raises so successfully each year in our sun-drenched porch.

The entertainment dates, like the visitors, thin out and the swallows gather in rows on the telephone wires, ready to go home.

November and I am off on a trip to Germany. This year it's Bavaria, at the request of a Pitlochry hotelier. As a released prisoner of war he elected to stay in

Scotland and fell in love with a Scottish girl but failed to get her parents' blessing.

However, one night, our Scots lass opened her bedroom window, threw out her hastily packed case, which burst open scattering the contents all over the neighbour's garden. The lassie floated after it into her sweetheart's arms and into a waiting taxi, whose driver witnessed their runaway marriage.

But the Bavarian was a man of purpose and vowed that, one day, he would give his bride a real wedding in his own country. On their twenty-fifth anniversary, in a Roman Catholic church in Bavaria, the wedding was re-enacted with myself best man and, high in the balcony near the roof on the church, Shona, one of our piping daughters, played Amazing Grace.

The haunting air pervaded the church, mingling with the masses of flowers with which the beautiful building was decorated.

After the service came the feasting and dancing that brought time to a standstill for a period of three days. We ate suckling pig washed down with champagne and danced to the oom-pa oom-pa of the bands. Bavarian dancing is the most exhausting exercise I have ever undertaken! I looked across at Shona who was going through all the prancing and armpumping motions with a handsome, young, racing driver.

"It is good", said the bridegroom.

"But," said I, "he has no English and Shona has no German".

"Love", said Hans, with a wealth of meaning and experience, "has no language barrier".

When December comes the year gets old and crotchety and its breath has a chill bite. But this doesn't frighten us. The barn is full of hay that holds on tightly to the sweet smell of summer and, stacked in the turnip shed, cuddled closely together, are the purple and golden balls of condensed sunshine and soft morning dews.

On the shelves in the outhouse are the apples and the nuts, the berries and the honey, all safely stored.

The last light of day, in a duck-egg blue sky, brings the call from the incoming wild geese. Our own gander stands on tiptoe, stretches his neck and answers, once, twice. It is time for action. The flock of greylags dip over the croft, their dark shapes now just visible and the fire flashes from my gun.

Manna never fell from Heaven with such a thump as this. One for the Christmas dinner and one for New Year and, from our own gander, one big hiss of relief!

Before Christmas there was yet another trip abroad, this time by invitation of the British Embassy in Bonn. It is for a British Week and they like me to bring a group of Pipers, Highland dancers, singers and accordionists to represent Scotland.

Our tour of Bonn savoured of something more than mere success. We appeared on television and for radio shows and we performed in the streets of Bonn and Bad Godesburg for the people. They flocked to listen and to follow us, especially one old lady, with a little folding stool which, when not in use, she tucked underneath her arm.

We also attended the glittering Embassy parties, so smoothly run with someone always with a finger on the pulse of events and a sense of timing to the next heart beat.

Our last evening was reserved for an appearance at a mammoth Wine Festival. A large wooden stage, reminiscent of a boxing ring, had been erected in the town square for the participants in the evening's festivities, particularly the oompa-oompa brass band.

THE KILT FOR KEEPS

Our task was to give them a much needed 'breather' for an hour.

It was a breathtaking moment, for me, to address this sea of humanity, thousand upon thousand of wine-sipping revellers, all waiting for something to happen. We made it happen, and finished by singing 'Scotland the Brave' with the backing of the pipes and accordions. This was too much for the multitude and the whole Square erupted. The wooden stage creaked, groaned and shifted about alarmingly as the waves of excited humanity swept forward to embrace us.

After our turn we escaped, with the help of the police, to join in the rest of the evening's festivities.

The wine must have been strengthening as I won my way to the finals of the arm-wrestling competition and found myself, once more, on the stage and facing Manfield, the big Bavarian, in the finals. He was sporting in defeat but stoutly maintained I had an advantage wearing the kilt, and I had the feeling he could have been right.

The Burgermaster presented me with my prize, a case of wine.

The crowds roared for more of the 'doodlesacs' so we gave it to them, together with their favourite 'pipe' tune, "Muss i Denn". There are certainly no wooden hearts around here and the stage rocked about like a ship in a storm. But, by now, we had got our 'sea legs' and, thanks to the quality of the wine, were a trifle care-free. Hanne, an artist from Trier, gave me a painting to 'hang in Scotland' where, she said, "My heart is".

I have learned by now what shepherding is all about and skilfully rounded up the pipers, accordionists, singer and dancers and pointed all their noses to home. It's just a jet step from one way of life to another.

Croft Douglas has a welcome all of its own, a special

something that reaches out to claim you. But all the news is not good.

Accident, age and arthritis had finally caught up with Tarra, our faithful collie, and her greeting was a feeble thump of the tail. I carried her, cradled in my arms, down to the lochside. She didn't mind the rifle and the spade slung on my back, she had seen them many times before, and her nose crinkled continuously as she smelt the ham bone in my pocket. Tarra was never fussy about her food but a ham bone, hot from the soup pot, was one of her favourites.

As I laid her down, she wrapped her tongue, lovingly, around the luscious, succulent, bone and never heard the rifle shot that banished all her pain. I put Tarra to rest at the feet of the Lady of the Woods, an elegant, silver birch that bowed her head and did the crying with little, leafy, tears that settled lightly on the freshly turned earth.

When I got back home, Irralee dried her tears and set off, purposefully, for Pitlochry. She returned with a little black and white Cocker Spaniel puppy, sat it down in front of me, saying,

"The rest of the litter were just puppies. But this one is for you, it's got character!"

I looked at the one black-patched eye that glittered from the darkness without letting anyone know what it was thinking. The other eye watched me straightforwardly from its white background, and its surrounding black spots spelled out honesty, in capital letters. The puppy ran round the room as if propelled by some magical dynamo charged, I was sure, by the little tail that wagged non-stop.

"What", asked Irralee, "are you going to call her?"

I took a deep breath and felt the pain lift from the day.

"That's Ceilidh. Definitely. Ceilidh".

And that night the new puppy accepted Croft Douglas as her home and settled in her bed without a whimper. Ceilidh was as independent as her spots. In no time at all she had us all licking her hairy paw! She brings the slippers when she thinks they are needed, her food bowl when she thinks it is coming up for feed time. She brings the letters and the newspaper from the postman and carries the shopping parcels. Carrying is her business.

Everyone speaks to Ceilidh, but it hasn't spoilt her, she accepts it as part of life. At the beginning she had a burning passion to pursue poultry, especially when they got hysterical and flapped about desperately. Ceilidh took her whacking without a murmur but, even today, when she tip-toes her way quietly through the flock, I am sure her eyes are tightly closed!

Ceilidh can count, too, She gets three biscuits for her supper. If I only put down two, she doesn't touch them, but gives a direct look from the white bordered eye while the black one darkly awaits the third. In the evening when we sit around the fire and the birch logs are blazing, Ceilidh loves to slip in behind me and share my chair. Irralee was knitting and I asked her,

"Did Cocker Spaniels originally come from Spain?"

"Some say so," she replied, with out looking up.

"Then", I said, "Ceilidh must have been a Princess in her last life".

That made Irralee raise her eyes above 'needle level'.

"A Princess?"

"Yes. She has just spoken to me", and when Ceilidh answers a question it is quite an experience. She gently pokes a moist nose in to your ear and, confidentially, blows once for "No", and twice for "Yes".

Irralee tried to escape by switching her concentration to counting stitches, but I was warming to the subject of reincarnation and about my visit to a Buddhist Temple in Copenhagen.

Religion I have always regarded as a wide open door and I wondered what message lay in the Temple. I followed the gentleman in front. He took off his shoes, so I followed his example. There was a strange hush, broken only by the whispering of burning incense. The man in front dropped to his knees before a gigantic Buddha seated majestically at the top of three marble steps, and bowed low. His jersey parted company with the top of his trousers and slid upwards to expose a pink portion of his back.

Out of respect I followed and bowed, too, but I knew the belt around my kilt would keep everything in order as far as those behind were concerned. I sat, cross-legged, on a little mat, as everyone else did, and did my best to empty out my mind and make a suitable receptacle for thoughts from a higher plane. They never got a chance to arrive. The alarm of my wrist watch went off.

It was a new fangled device that played a stirring rendering of 'Scotland the Brave'. The watch was new to me, and I new to it. I punched desperately at every protruding plunger, to no avail. Finally, I stuffed it in the pleats of my kilt where it sounded as if the pipe band were now playing in the distance. But still my watch held everyone's attention and played havoc with their session of meditation.

I was forced to make a hurried exit, bowing apologetically to the Buddha on my way out. I was sure, as I fled past, that the Buddha's Big Bounteous Belly was shaken by a sudden spiritual spasm of mirth.

Irralee takes her mirth more seriously. She starts to laugh but switches to a series of 'oho, oho, oho', the tears stream from her eyes and she holds her sides together in delightful agony. Quiet is only restored when

211

I disappear and return with a cup of hot chocolate and Irralee's favourite snack — toast, spread thickly with marmalade.

That year came one of the severest winters we had ever experienced. In mid-December a thin wind blew from the north-east, it stayed just where it was and grew colder and colder. It tired of just being cold and turned to meaner tactics, throwing blizzards of snow, whipping up the fallen flakes to a furious frenzy, sending them down again in swirling whirlwinds.

It lined the valley and happed it up in a deep, white blanket, whistled up and down surveying the havoc it had caused and, in an expansive mood, decided to rest. His partner, the frost, who had been asleep all this time, woke suddenly and, appreciating the quiet, laid an icy hand over the land with an iron grip that grew tighter every night. The decorative ferns that had grown so delicately across the windows, grew to thick bunches of arctic proportions.

During the ominous silence I reminded myself that, only last August, I had swum across the loch and decided that, next morning, I would call the Big Bluff, and walk across. And I did. But it didn't make any difference to the frost.

Food and fuel were getting low and we were anxiously counting the bales of hay in the barn. In the shelter of the house we can do without, but those outside must have food to survive. Every winter, prior to this one, the Highland Cattle had been given a meal of hay in the morning, but this year, for the first time, there was a lowing of distress when darkness fell. A message, that in the day's foraging, they had found nothing, not even a piece of frozen moss to supplement their breakfast. The bovine talk rumbled with fear. The fear that the night will be too cold, that they with empty bellies will succumb and will lie, upturned, to meet the dawn.

I set out through the snow, floundering through the drifts, whose icy crusts cut cruelly into my bare knees, balancing a precious bale of hay on my back. All at once, there was a mass of milling, hungry, hairy bodies all around me and I quickly threw out the leaves of hay. As I turned to escape the sweeping, scything horns the deep snow treacherously gripped my legs. There was no direct menace from the animals, just a desperate anxiety to get to the food, but, duck and dodge as much as I could, I was struck in my side with the point of a horn.

It was my friend, Drumbuie, with his five-foot span, but I knew that in his big, Highland heart he meant me no harm. Accidents happen and, as I freed myself from the snow trap, I immediately forgave him. My cracked ribs were not so forgiving and gave me no sleep. So I was banished to the spare bedroom, where I could continue to whisper and whine whilst searching for a position that would afford relief.

How I muttered in my torment, how are we going to get the cattle fed?

How often we worry about tomorrow, when so often it takes care of itself, or, at least, someone else does.

In the morning, Irralee produced her solution to the problem. The children's sledge! It served admirably for towing out the bales and tipping them off smartly before the stampede started.

It was bitterly cold, even the trees seemed frozen to death. The cattle moved around like sleep-walking ghosts, trailing long icicles that touched the ground to swing and tinkle with each other. A cock chaffinch tumbled in front of us and expired with a last flutter, lying on its back, eyes closed and beak wide open in a final protest at having to die of cold and hunger. It would never, now, sing in the spring. But would Spring ever come? Would this all embracing, deadly, chill never release its stranglehold on the land?

The answer was in the wind as it suddenly changed into the West. The earth and everything in it dared to breathe freely again and even the butterflies on the Croft Douglas ceilings risked the occasional sleep-walk. But the loch was in torment, moaning, groaning and growling fearsomely. The ice was locked in a contest of life or death with the warmth from the West. There were loud, terrifying explosions as the ice rent itself apart to build up a barricade as a last defence.

The West wind laughed, knowing that this would only end as an act of self destruction and, watching as the huge jagged floes reared up to crash against each other, before pressing forward again with the rippling waters in its wake, demonstrating, once and for all, that the soft, warm, gentle approach of the West Wind will always prevail.

Next morning the snow plough was growling, too, but in a friendly manner, as it bit huge chunks out of the snow drifts and opened up the road to bring us, once again, into contact with the outside world.

It was a morning to breathe in deeply and savour its taste. On the spur of the moment I decided to climb to the top of Creag Mhor (Big Rock) that stands at the back of Croft Douglas. My ribs still hurt but the pain became secondary and was forgotten as I reached the top and looked down. Every step of the climb had been worth while.

The kiss of the rising sun brought a hazy, purple blush to the tips of the silver birches and something for the missel thrush to sing about. The waters of the loch were rolling lazily at the foot of majestic Schiehallion.

Down at Croft Douglas the cockerel was crowing, rejoicing with his flock at the first trip into the open for six weeks.

Shall I keep looking down and scratch with the chickens, or raise my eyes and fly with the eagle? There he is gliding effortlessly over the top of Creag-an-loch.

The westerly breeze, tugging playfully at the pleats of my kilt, reminds me of the kilts I have outgrown and handed down to start life all over again, and of what my daughter told me; how her little boy had been at school and some of the bigger boys were ragging him about his kilt. But the wee lad had stood his ground and silenced the opposition, by stoutly declaring,

"My Grandad always wore one. So it MUST be all right".

With a faith and a following like that, it just had to be the kilt for keeps.